ROUTLEDGE LIBRARY EDITIONS: AMERICA – REVOLUTION & CIVIL WAR

Volume 4

LINCOLN AND THE AMERICAN CIVIL WAR

LINCOLN AND THE AMERICAN CIVIL WAR

AUDREY CAMMIADE

LONDON AND NEW YORK

First published in Great Britain in 1967 by Methuen

This edition first published in 2021
by Routledge
2 Park Square, Milton Park, Abingdon, Oxon OX14 4RN

and by Routledge
52 Vanderbilt Avenue, New York, NY 10017

Routledge is an imprint of the Taylor & Francis Group, an informa business

© 1967 Audrey Cammiade

All rights reserved. No part of this book may be reprinted or reproduced or utilised in any form or by any electronic, mechanical, or other means, now known or hereafter invented, including photocopying and recording, or in any information storage or retrieval system, without permission in writing from the publishers.

Trademark notice: Product or corporate names may be trademarks or registered trademarks, and are used only for identification and explanation without intent to infringe.

British Library Cataloguing in Publication Data
A catalogue record for this book is available from the British Library

ISBN: 978-0-367-54033-3 (Set)
ISBN: 978-1-00-312459-7 (Set) (ebk)
ISBN: 978-0-367-64065-1 (Volume 4) (hbk)
ISBN: 978-1-00-312219-7 (Volume 4) (ebk)

Publisher's Note
The publisher has gone to great lengths to ensure the quality of this reprint but points out that some imperfections in the original copies may be apparent.

This book is a re-issue originally published in 1967. The language used is a reflection of its era and no offence is meant by the Publishers to any reader by this re-publication.

Disclaimer
The publisher has made every effort to trace copyright holders and would welcome correspondence from those they have been unable to trace.

LINCOLN
AND THE
AMERICAN CIVIL WAR

Lincoln in 1860

LINCOLN
AND THE
AMERICAN CIVIL WAR

by Audrey Cammiade

Maps by R. R. Sellman

ROY PUBLISHERS, INC · NEW YORK 10021

© 1967 Audrey Cammiade

Library of Congress No. 66-13355

Printed in Great Britain

CONTENTS

UNITY	*page*	8
SLAVERY		8
THE TERRITORIES		11
THE RISE OF LINCOLN		14
THE GREAT DEBATES		15
THE PRESIDENCY		17
THE COMING OF WAR – FORT SUMTER		19
SPRING AND SUMMER 1861 – BULL RUN		22
LATE SUMMER 1861 – FRÉMONT IN MISSOURI		26
THE END OF 1861 – THE "TRENT" AFFAIR		27
NEW YEAR, 1862 – NO MORE OYSTERS IN THE POTOMAC		29
SPRING, 1862 – MOVEMENT ON THE MISSISSIPPI		31
MARCH TO APRIL, 1862 – THE "MERRIMAC" AND THE "MONITOR"		34
MCCLELLAN ON THE PENINSULA		36
AUGUST, 1862 – SECOND BATTLE OF BULL RUN		40
SEPTEMBER, 1862 – ANTIETAM		42
THE EMANCIPATION OF THE SOUTHERN SLAVES		45
DECEMBER, 1862 – FREDERICKSBURG		48
EARLY 1863 – CHANCELLORSVILLE		49

CONTENTS

	page
JULY, 1863 – GETTYSBURG	53
1863 – THE WESTERN THEATRE	58
AUTUMN IN TENNESSEE	59
JUSTICE OR MERCY?	60
UNAHAPPY NEW YEAR, 1864	62
MAY, 1864 – GRANT IN THE WILDERNESS	64
JUNE – COLD HARBOR	66
AUTUMN, 1864 – GRANT AT PETERSBURG	66
SUMMER, 1864 – SHERMAN'S MARCH THROUGH GEORGIA	68
THE *Alabama* AND MOBILE – TWO TRIUMPHS FOR THE NAVY	69
SHERIDAN IN THE SHENANDOAH – A TRIUMPH FOR THE CAVALRY	70
ELECTIONS	71
1865 – THE END OF SLAVERY	74
1865 – THE END OF THE WAR	75
1865 – THE END OF THE PRESIDENT	81
THOSE THAT WERE LEFT	82
THE STRICKEN SOUTH	84
Order of Events	89
A Select Book List	91
Index	93

LINCOLN AND THE CIVIL WAR

To create an ideal form of government is all very well provided you can also create the men to be governed and the country they are to live in. The Founding Fathers who drew up the Constitution of the United States had to take the men and the country ready-made. As delegates of all the thirteen original States except Rhode Island, they met in Philadelphia in 1787 to "revise the Articles of Confederation", but found themselves involved in an even bigger task. What they really did was to weld the States into one nation.

It was difficult because the States were so unalike. Their climates were different, for they were strung out over more than a thousand miles of coastline. They had been colonised at different times and for different reasons. They were different in size and in strength, in soil and in ways of living.

The most northerly had a hardworking, puritanical population mainly from England. Winters were cold there and life was strenuous; industries were growing fast. But in the South the planters lived the easy, spacious lives of country gentlefolk, with Negro slaves to do most of the manual work. Between these two extremes was a land of mixed races, of small farms and thriving towns. Merchants and professional men and shipbuilders could have very much the same kind of social life as they would have had in western Europe. Negro slaves were much rarer there than in the South, but there were plenty of indentured servants – men and women whose passages from Europe had been paid for them by their employers, and who were still working off their debt.

Beyond all this, to the west, were enormous regions still to be developed. Farms were being hacked out of the primeval forest by families of settlers – men, women and children working to the limits of their strength. Soap, candles and cloth were not bought from shops in those parts, but made by the women in their log cabins. Meat did not come from a butcher but was stalked by father – or perhaps by mother – with a gun. This great hinterland had to be borne very much in mind, for as time went on it, too, would become part of the Union.

Unity

The people of all these regions could not be expected to live in exactly the same way or obey exactly the same laws. Each State drew up its own Constitution. Within limits it dealt with things like roadmaking, education, crime and punishment, as suited it best. What the Founding Fathers had to do was to provide a central Constitution for them all, and to set up a Federal Government that would control the things by which all of them were affected. Customs duties, postal services, the Army and Navy, foreign affairs – these must be controlled on behalf of the whole country, by representatives of the whole country. And certain individual rights must be assured to every citizen, no matter what State he belonged to. So the Constitution was drawn up, in the name of "the People", as a solemn contract, entered into by every citizen on behalf of himself and his descendants.

If individual States were to break the contract and set up on their own, then, as the Founding Fathers saw it, those States would destroy themselves and each other. They would go to war just as neighbouring countries in Europe went to war. Each would have to keep a standing army of its own, at a great sacrifice of money and personal liberty; and the weaker would still be in danger from the stronger, the stronger in danger from outside attack. Whatever happened, the Union must stay united. This was an article of faith for future Americans, among them Abraham Lincoln.

Between 1789, when the Constitution went into effect, and the outbreak of the Civil War, several States did consider breaking away – seceding, as it was called. But the Union held good and no State did actually secede, until December 1860.

Slavery

The Founding Fathers had to accept slavery whether they liked it or not. Some admitted privately that they did not like it at all, but they could not simply do away with it by law. The Southern States had depended on it for about a hundred and fifty years, and would certainly refuse to join a Union in which it was forbidden. Accordingly, the Fathers, without using the word "slavery", laid down that if "a person held to service" in one State escaped to another, he was to be "delivered up on claim of the party to whom such service or labour might be due". In other words, runaway slaves were to be handed back to their masters. Nothing was said about who was responsible for handing them back: and later on Governors of non-slave States were apt to say that this was no duty of theirs – the Federal Government must see to it.

The Constitution also declared that after the end of 1807 Congress might prevent "the imigration or importation" of certain classes of "persons". Congress did, in fact, make the slave-trade illegal after that date. So shipbuilders and ship-owners could no longer make fortunes out of it – at least, not openly. Many did very well out of it in secret. In theory, sea captains could be put to death for it: in practice, not one of them was, until Abraham Lincoln, as President, decided not to reprieve a contraband slave-trader called Gordon. Lincoln, most merciful of men, was widely blamed for this piece of "brutality".

Perhaps Lincoln was right in his belief that the Founding Fathers counted on slavery's dying out of its own accord. But nothing of the sort happened. In 1790 there were about 700,000 slaves in the Union: in 1860 there were about 3,500,000, and South Carolina had two Negroes to every white. But there were far fewer in the North, and those few were free. The Northern climate, and the Northerners' work, were less suitable for them. Besides, white workers were pouring in from Europe, and did not want slave labour to compete with. The North not only did not want the Negro as a slave: it did not want him at all. But the South felt it couldn't carry on without him.

The Southern planter would point out that his Negroes were better fed, better cared for, safer and happier than the factory workers of the North. He gave them meat and corn, shoes in winter, cabins to live in, and medical treatment when they were ill. They could not marry without his consent – but he usually consented, because he liked them to marry and have children, since the children were also his property. They might be beaten – but they were seldom beaten severely, because he liked them to be fit for work. They might have long hours – but so had the factory hands. They might be kept ignorant, and indeed in South Carolina it was unlawful to teach them to read – but children seldom complain of not having lessons, and grown Negroes in those days were often very like children. They might be too dependent on their owner's will – but the big plantation-owner, as

A slave auction

a rule, was not a brute. He was often a very pleasant person indeed. He naturally preferred to be surrounded by gaiety and affection, if he could afford it.

It was when he could not afford it that his Negroes' troubles were worst. In her famous novel, *Uncle Tom's Cabin*, published in the 1850s, Harriet Beecher Stowe described the sufferings of helpless slaves whose master had to sell them. They were bundled off in chains to slave-markets like cattle, or like men guilty of hideous crime. Families were often separated and small children made to work for strangers. Young girls were publicly humiliated as auctioneers showed them off to the crowd, commenting on their beauty or strength. And though extreme cruelty was punishable by law, a Negro could not give evidence in court against a white man, even in free States such as Illinois. If he were ill-treated, he had to put up with it unless another white man chose to intervene.

The Territories

Meanwhile the Union was expanding to the west and south. In 1803, by the Louisiana Purchase, it bought from France an enormous territory stretching from the Gulf of Mexico to the Canadian border. Later it acquired another huge chunk in the south-west as the result of a short war with Mexico. These lands had to be settled and developed and then, as their populations grew, admitted bit by bit to the Union. For instance, out of part of the Louisiana Purchase were carved the two new States of Arkansas and Missouri. These two became slave States because of their position and climate, but the fate of the lands to the north of them had to be decided. Should slavery be allowed there, or should it not? In 1820 a statesman called Henry Clay suggested the "Missouri Compromise", by which there should be no slavery in the newly acquired country north of the parallel 36° 40′. This parallel is, in fact, the southern boundary of Missouri itself, but the Compromise did not affect the State, which had already been dealt with.

So far, so good: but the question soon cropped up again. The new land was being populated fast. Many slaveowners wanted to move in, taking their Negroes with them. At the same time, those who stayed in Missouri complained that they were now surrounded on three sides by "free" country to which their slaves could easily escape. And once gone, they were gone for ever. A chain of anti-slavery enthusiasts was ready to shelter them, passing them from family to family and smuggling them in due course over the border into Canada. So the South wanted the Missouri Compromise done away with. The time was coming when two more States would be formed in that area – Kansas and Nebraska. The argument was reopened. Should Kansas and Nebraska be slave States, or free?

The North insisted that they should be free, partly on moral grounds, partly because the poorer Northerners objected very much to seeing the work they wanted for themselves performed by unpaid labour.

In 1850 Clay again tried to solve the problem, without much success. It was becoming more and more urgent. Politicians and businessmen, including the astute Stephen Douglas, who was both, had schemes for Kansas and Nebraska, and wanted to see them achieve statehood and forge ahead. Douglas suggested that the people of the two future States should themselves decide by vote whether to allow slavery or not. He got a Bill to that effect through Congress. Then there was a wild race between North and South to send enough settlers – especially into Kansas – to sway the vote. There was rioting and violence and a certain amount of bloodshed. Five anti-slavery men were killed, and a fiery Northerner named John Brown set out to avenge them. Four of his sons helped him to drag five victims from their cabins and hack them to death with cutlasses. They turned out not to be pro-slavery agitators at all, but that was too bad. John Brown had simply acted as the spirit moved him.

Brown was heard of again a year later, when he tried to rouse the Negroes of Virginia to revolt. He and some twenty followers raided the United States arsenal at Harper's Ferry, fifty miles or so from Washington. They killed a Negro railway employee this time. Brown was duly caught and hanged, but the North made a hero of him. During the Civil War a Federal Army was to spread destruction in the South, singing as it went:

> *John Brown's body lies a-mouldering in the grave,*
> *But his soul goes marching on.*

Two more incidents show how tempers were roused over the slavery question. A Negro called Dred Scott was taken by his owner to live in a free State, and it was claimed that he could not legally be carted back to Missouri and re-enslaved. The case came before Chief Justice Taney, who ruled that Scott, like other slaves, had "no rights that the white man was bound to respect" and "might lawfully be treated as an ordinary article of merchandise and traffic whenever a profit could be made by it". A famous abolitionist, William Lloyd Garrison, declared that if the Dred Scott decision accorded with the Constitution, the Constitution was "a covenant with death and an agreement with hell". The fact that Scott was soon bought, freed, and installed in a decent job, did not alter what had been said.

Then a Senator, Charles Sumner, made a violently offensive speech about certain slaveowners. He refused to hear the other side of the question, declaring that there *was* no other side. So a nephew of one of the slaveowners caught him in the Senate when it was almost deserted, and bashed him over the head and back with a cane, so mercilessly that he was an invalid for the next five years. The young man

John Brown on the way to his execution

was much applauded for what he had done. He himself said at last that he was tired of being a hero to every bully in the South.

In short, both sides had their heroes – or bullies, whichever way you looked at it. The 1850s were troubled times in America. And in those years Americans first became familiar with the name of Abraham Lincoln.

The Rise of Lincoln

Lincoln was born in 1809 in Kentucky and grew up on a series of farms in the pioneer States of the Middle West. He was good with his fists and good with an axe, but not much use with a gun. He did not seem to like killing things. Local boys accepted him as a leader, partly because he was strong and partly because he was fun. He had only about twelve months' schooling, and there were very few books in his home. He made the most of them. The Bible, in particular, must have helped to form his mind, for his great speeches as President had a stately, biblical ring to them. But he always liked to tell funny stories in the pungent American of the Middle West, and to the end of his life he pronounced "chair" as "cheer" and tended to begin a sentence with a long, reflective "Wa-a-al".

Politics interested him. As a leggy, shabby, almost penniless young man, he was elected to the State Legislature of Illinois, and soon became one of its most enterprising members. He also studied law on his own, passed the necessary examinations, and built up a flourishing law practice. The next step was Congress. He got himself elected, and took his seat in 1847, when the slavery disputes were raging hot and strong.

Lincoln disapproved of slavery. His basic objection to it was simply that it was wrong. Even so, he was not in sympathy with the abolitionists, who wanted to make a clean sweep of it at once throughout the Union. He could see that that would ruin the slaveowners, and furthermore it would ruin the slaves. They would be turned loose in hundreds of thousands, without any idea of self-discipline and without any place prepared for them in any community. Finally, it would be unconstitutional. Lincoln's reverence for the Constitution went very deep.

With his mind alive to the difficulties, he kept fairly quiet in Congress. He watched and pondered and did not draw much attention to himself. He spoke against attempts to change the Constitution: "Better not take the first step, which may lead to the habit of altering it." His term came to an end in 1849, and back he went to Springfield, Illinois, to devote himself to his practice as a lawyer.

The Great Debates

Meanwhile there had been some shuffling of political parties. Two main ones had emerged – Democrats and Republicans. The two great parties of today have the same names, but different ideas behind them. Broadly speaking, the Democrats wanted strong State Governments and were divided about slavery, while the Republicans wanted a strong Federal Government and opposed slavery. Stephen Douglas, the framer of the Kansas-Nebraska Bill, was a Democrat. He stood for election to the Senate, and Lincoln agreed to oppose him as Republican candidate. Douglas was well known throughout the Union: Lincoln almost unknown outside Illinois. However, Douglas respected Lincoln as a strong adversary, and the duel between them caused enormous excitement, not only in Illinois, where it took place, but far beyond.

In one speech Lincoln said that the slavery dispute was working up to a crisis. "A house divided against itself cannot stand. I believe this Government cannot endure permanently half slave and half free. I do not expect the Union to be dissolved – I do not expect the house to fall – but I do expect that it will cease to be divided." Douglas declared that Lincoln was advocating a war between North and South, "a war of extermination to be continued until . . . all the States shall either become free or become slave". That was not what Lincoln advocated; at least, it was not what he wanted. But it was what was going to happen.

Lincoln objected to the Kansas-Nebraska act because it allowed in principle for the extension of slavery. Douglas said that it would not in practice extend it. Even if the anti-slavery men in Kansas and Nebraska were voted down, they could, when they were strong enough, bring in regulations to make slavery so impractical that it would die out. By saying this, he laid up a lot of trouble for himself and for his party. The Democrats of the South suspected that he was against slavery at heart: the Democrats of the North accused him of being pro-slavery. And although

Lincoln speaking in the Great Debates. Stephen Douglas is standing behind him

he won that election and became a Senator, he split his party and ruined his hopes of ever being President.

With Lincoln it was just the opposite. He lost that election and was never a Senator, but he helped his party make up its mind and established himself as one of its greatest leaders. He stirred up those who were apathetic about slavery, but he still firmly refused to join the abolitionists. He knew when to use eloquence and when to use wit and when to use hard common sense. Republicans everywhere invited him to speak, and newspapers everywhere reported what he had said.

The Presidency

Since the Democrats were split, it seemed that the Republicans had only to agree on the choice of their own candidate and he would be elected President in November, 1860. They held a convention in Chicago to pick their man. To be nominated, he would have to gain more than half of the Convention's votes. If nobody did this at the first ballot – and as a rule nobody did – there would be a second, a third, and so on, until somebody had an absolute majority. Between ballots there would be much bargaining, the supporters of one candidate agreeing to vote for another if something were promised in return.

Lincoln was one of the strongest candidates. That meant that he had to stay away; but he warned his friends that he did not authorise any bargains and would not feel bound by any that were made. They made some all the same – they could not have got him nominated without – and he did, in fact, stand by their word. His greatest rival, Seward, was defeated chiefly because the next strongest, Chase and Cameron, lost many votes to Lincoln on the second and third ballots. So Lincoln was the Republican candidate: and he knew that his chances of beating Stephen Douglas to the Presidency were pretty good. When November came he had 1,866,452 votes, and Douglas 1,376,957.

There remained the problem of what to do with Seward, Chase and Cameron. Lincoln offered to make Seward Secretary of State – a post corresponding to Britain's Foreign Secretary. Seward hesitated, accepted, and became a very valuable colleague and a close friend. Chase was a distinguished, high-minded, but somewhat difficult person, who had made a strong stand against slavery and devoted a great deal of his own money to buying up slaves and freeing them. Lincoln honoured his supporters' promises by giving Chase the Secretaryship of the Treasury, a post Chase was well able to fill. Cameron was a more awkward proposition. People warned Lincoln that Cameron was not to be trusted. They gave him no proofs, though: and so Lincoln quelled his own doubts and made Cameron Secretary for War.

This last appointment was to turn out disastrously. When war came, as it soon did,

Cameron made enormous profits for his friends out of army contracts, and soldiers were provided with the shoddiest boots, uniforms and knapsacks, which came unstuck as soon as rained on. An outspoken Congressman, Thaddeus Stevens, aired his views about Cameron to Lincoln. Lincoln asked Stevens if he thought Cameron would actually steal, to which Stevens replied that he did not think Cameron would steal a red-hot stove. This remark got round to Cameron, who demanded that Stevens should withdraw it. Stevens said cheerfully, to Lincoln, "I believe I told you he would *not* steal a red-hot stove. I now take that back".

Other appointments were not quite so important and not quite so worrying, but the sheer number of them harrassed Lincoln from the moment of his election. There were four months before he would actually take office. During those four months he was besieged by wire-pullers, place-seekers and fanatics of every kind. He disliked saying "no", but he had to say it again and again. At the same time, abolitionists were imploring him to take a firm line over slavery and not to put up with any nonsense from the South, while peace-lovers were beseeching him to reassure the Southerners and promise to protect the slaveowners' rights. Lincoln replied that he had already given his views on slavery often and publicly. If he now repeated that it would be unconstitutional to interfere with slavery in States where it was lawful, the South would take that as a confession of weakness: but if he gave in to the abolitionists, and condemned slavery, there would be war. He would say nothing. Once he exclaimed in desperation, "I am sick of office-holding already".

In February 1861 he travelled to Washington to take over from Buchanan, the outgoing President. It was a long journey, with many stops for public receptions and speechmaking. The last such stop was to be at Baltimore, capital of Maryland, a slave State where trouble was brewing. A private detective agency, and several worried friends, warned him that there was a plot to assassinate him and that he had better not arrive in Baltimore by the scheduled private train. He was no coward, but it would be disastrous for the country if he were murdered before even taking office. So he reached Baltimore by ordinary express some hours before he was expected. This was necessary. Still, it threw out the arrangements for his reception, gave enemies a chance to sneer, and made a poor beginning.

Washington turned out to hear his inaugural address. It had been a difficult one

Emaciated slaves at the American market

to compose. The Union by now was splitting, and seven Southern States had already broken away. He tried to reason with the secessionists. "The Government will not assail you," he declared. "You can have no conflict, without being yourselves the aggressors. You can have no oath registered in heaven to destroy the Government, while *I* shall have the most solemn one, to preserve, protect and maintain it."

The Coming of War – Fort Sumter

In spite of all Lincoln had said, the Southerners had seen his election as a catastrophe, and South Carolina, which had threatened to secede if he became President, kept its word. In December 1860, South Carolina left the Union. Mississippi, Florida,

Alabama, Georgia and Louisiana had followed in January 1861, and Texas in February.

The map shows that these seven States are neighbours in the south-eastern corner of the mainland. They were known as the "Cotton States", because cotton was what they lived by: they sold huge quantities of it to other countries,

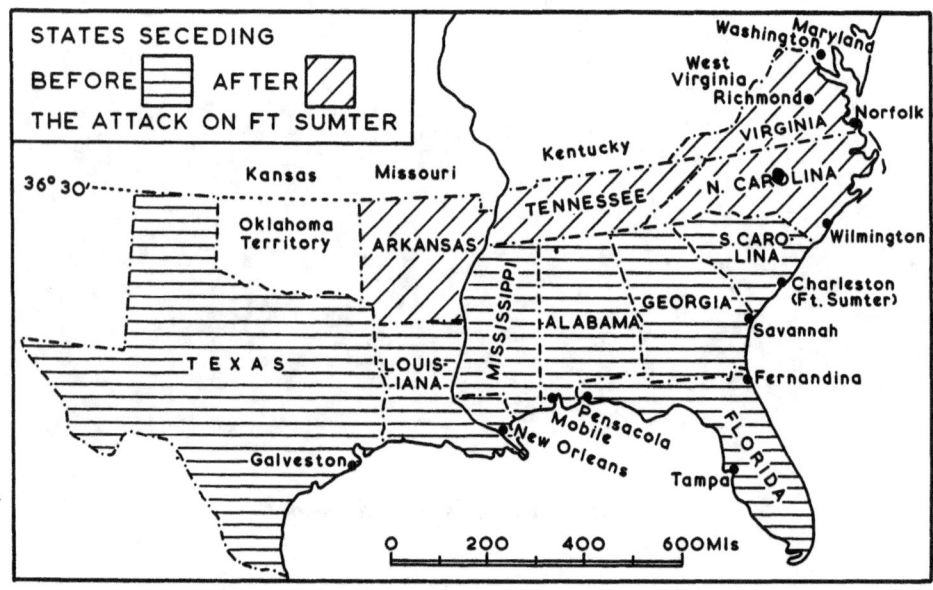

Map I

especially Britain. They hoped that in their quarrel with the Federal Government Britain would back them up. Together they set up their own Confederation, with Jefferson Davis as their President; and they would thereafter be known as the Confederates, the Northerners as Federals.

All this happened while Buchanan was still in office. He was an ineffectual old gentleman, much worried, as well he might be, and longing for his release. Almost all he did about the situation was to try rather feebly to reinforce Fort Sumter, one of three Federal forts in Charleston Harbour, South Carolina. His attempt failed: the Confederates fired on the relief ship and turned it back.

The main battery at Fort Sumter

Anderson, the officer in charge of all three forts, abandoned two and moved their garrisons to Fort Sumter, where they held on in spite of dwindling supplies.

As soon as he took over Lincoln notified the Governor of South Carolina that he was sending a shipload of provisions to the fort. Anderson announced that he could not hold out after April 15th unless the provisions arrived. Until then he would not surrender, though the Confederates called on him to do so. On the 13th the Confederates opened fire. He retaliated as best he could, but on the 14th he had to give in, not through loss of lives – for nobody was killed – but through hunger and exhaustion. He and his men were allowed to march out with the honours of war.

From that time on Lincoln treated the Confederates as rebels. The term was used by the Northerners in speaking of them. They had fired the first shots, and there was no longer any question of conciliation. Lincoln called out 75,000 militiamen, appropriated money for the Army and Navy, and ordered a blockade of the

The interior of Fort Sumter after bombardment

Southern ports. Thereupon Virginia, which had been wavering, joined the Confederates, and Arkansas, North Carolina and Tennessee followed suit. There were loyal Unionists in all these States. Indeed, North-West Virginia refused to go along with the rest and seceded from the secessionists. Organised by a young major-general called McClellan, her people took their own line, and in due course West Virginia became part of the Union as a State in her own right.

Spring and Summer, 1861 – Bull Run

Now the Confederates had eleven States on their side with something like 9,000,000 people including 3,500,000 Negroes. They had only one big factory turning out heavy armaments, and relied mainly on what they could capture from the Federals or buy from abroad. The Federals, on the other hand, had twenty-three States plus West Virginia and about 22,000,000 people. They also had control of the Navy, plenty of factories, a better railway system than the South, and much more money.

But the South had the finer generals. By common consent, the nation's best soldier was Robert E. Lee, and Lincoln sent for him at once. Unfortunately Lee was a Virginian. With obvious sorrow he said he could not fight against his own State, and rode off across the Potomac to join Jefferson Davis at Richmond. The Federal High command was left with General Winfield Scott, a veteran of the Mexican war, too old and infirm now to sit a horse.

In spite of their superior resources, the Federals were in danger for a week or two of losing their capital city. Washington stands in the District of Columbia, bounded on three sides by Maryland and on the fourth by the Potomac River. Across the river lies Virginia. Virginia, of course, was enemy country, and Maryland, which was a slave State, seemed very likely to turn Confederate, too. That would mean that Washington would be cut off from the rest of the Union. As it was, secessionists wrecked railways and telegraph lines leading from Washington through Baltimore to the North, and a Massachusetts regiment, coming to Washington's defence, was attacked by a Baltimore mob, so that it struggled through at the cost of seventeen wounded. For many days no more troops arrived – and the Confederate headquarters at Richmond were uncomfortably near.

But another route through Maryland was found, and more men streamed into the capital. By the end of April Washington had a defence force of about 10,000. Then the Federal General Butler installed himself near Baltimore, and the secessionists quieted down. In two more months Maryland and her neighbour Delaware seemed safe for the Union.

So much for defence, but defence was not enough. The Northerners poured men, money and supplies into Washington and expected results. They chafed because a Confederate force held Harper's Ferry (the scene of John Brown's exploit) and the important railway junction of Manassas just south of it. Impatient politicians clamoured for action. Lincoln was accused, by Seward among others, of having no policy and of letting things slide.

Harper's Ferry was soon cleared – the Confederates withdrew from it under threat of an attack – and Lincoln consulted Winfield Scott about dislodging them from Manassas. The old man demurred. He said that the troops needed more training. Lincoln overbore his objections, and put the local force – the Army of the Potomac – under General McDowell, a younger, fitter man. McDowell also asked for more time to drill his men, but Lincoln pointed out that many had been called up for three months only and must be used now or released without having struck a blow. If they were green, he said, so were the Confederates.

It was true that the Confederates were inexperienced soldiers, but most of them could ride and shoot, and were not quite such raw material as the factory hands of the North. In the battle of Bull Run, near Manassas, the Federals got the worst of it. Though neither side could exactly claim a victory, the Northerners had great cause to rue defeat. Next day, tired, discouraged soldiers straggled into Washington without order and in many cases without equipment. It was the first real battle of the war; much had been hoped from it; and it came as a bitter disappointment. Lincoln, sad and shaken, spent as much time as he could in the camps round Washington, trying to cheer the men.

McDowell was moved to another command and replaced at the head of the Army of the Potomac by McClellan, fresh from success in West Virginia. Presently Winfield Scott retired and McClellan was given the supreme command. He was a good trainer and disciplinarian and popular with his men, but he had two failings – he always overestimated the enemy, and he always felt that he was being misjudged and ill-used by those above him. Lincoln treated him tactfully. He provided him with plenty of money, food and men, and strove to reassure him, pointing out that the Confederates were not as strong as he supposed. Senators showed rising impatience, and the General cried, "Don't let them hurry me." Lincoln thought of Bull Run. He did not want to repeat that mistake. He promised that McClellan should have his way.

The summer was passing into a fine, dry autumn, perfect for fighting; and yet McClellan did not fight. He proceeded efficiently with his training. The trouble was that the Confederates were training, too, and were left almost unhampered. "All quiet on the Potomac" had been a cry of relief when Washington was in real danger: it became a sneer when Washington was stiff with soldiers doing nothing but exercise. Lincoln realised that it was only too common for civilians to expect raw recruits to be turned into first-class troops overnight. He was patient. At last McClellan ordered a very minor raid. It failed. A small Federal force was defeated at Ball's Bluff and its leader, a personal friend of Lincoln's, was killed. Lincoln was grief-stricken, but McClellan seemed to shrug the thing off.

Lincoln's responsibilities were unbearably heavy. He was the head of the armed forces as well as the political head of the nation. He could be consulted about anything, asked for anything, blamed for anything. He deliberately made himself approachable because that was his nature and he thought it better so. He comforted numberless unfortunates, prevented numberless little harshnesses and injustices, and became known, not as a remote figure of authority, but as a warmly human person.

Lincoln and McClellan in conference

But the strain was terrific. He listened to every hothead, every malcontent and every arm-chair strategist, and sometimes responded with a funny story because it was no use trying to explain the truth. Quarrels between Ministers and Senators were legion, and he was drawn into them all. It sometimes seemed as though the only person who wouldn't confide in him was McClellan. He had to beg McClellan to tell him his plans, and McClellan was often evasive to the point of rudeness. One story goes to illustrate the relationship between them. McClellan was once so irritated by the President's pleas for detailed information that he sent him a sarcastic telegram announcing that he had captured two cows. What was he to do with them? The President wired back, "Milk them, George."

Late Summer, 1861 – Frémont in Missouri

When Lincoln's subordinates did act without consulting him, there was generally trouble. He had given command of the Federal forces in Missouri to Frémont, a celebrated explorer. Frémont had big ideas: he spoke grandly of his plans for the future, but did little in the present except to spend money. Reports came in of his injustices, extravagance and inertia. In August he allowed a small Federal detachment to be defeated with much slaughter by a Confederate one of twice its size. It was generally thought that he could have prevented this if he had only bestirred himself.

Yet Lincoln hesitated to interfere. Frémont was a picturesque figure: he had a big following: and his job was difficult. Missouri was a slave State, and though officially it was loyal to the Union, many of its inhabitants sympathised with the South and harassed the Union troops by guerrilla warfare. To punish these Frémont proclaimed that all Missouri citizens who fought against the Union would forfeit their property, including their slaves, who would automatically become free.

The proclamation was an embarrassment to Lincoln. He had to think not only of Missouri, but of other slave States whose loyalty he was struggling to keep – Maryland, Delaware, and Kentucky. Even in the District of Columbia itself, slavery was permitted and slaveowners were very touchy. Many soldiers from these areas threw down their arms in disgust, saying that they were not fighting to free a lot of Negroes. Lincoln saw their point. He insisted that the war was a war to preserve the Union, not to abolish slavery, and in any case it was not for Frémont to make political decisions of that kind. So Frémont got a letter from the President, asking him to modify his edict. There was no response. Lincoln waited a little longer, to see if Frémont showed any signs of winning a battle, and finally relieved him of his command. It was an unpleasant thing to have to do, and it raised a storm among Frémont's admirers and among vigorous anti-slave men such as Charles Sumner.

The End of 1861 – The "Trent" Affair

The confederates had counted from the first on the sympathy of England. Their

Shooting cotton bales into a river steamer on the Alabama

raw cotton fed the English mills, and their easy, graceful manners appealed to the English mind. And England's help would be priceless to the Confederacy. With it, the blockade of the Southern ports could be broken, and the Southern soldiers could be properly armed.

Accordingly, the Confederates chose two agents called Mason and Slidell, and packed them off from the neutral port of Havana on a British Royal Mail Packet, the *Trent*.

On November 8th, when the *Trent* was in the Bahama Channel, she was stopped by a shot across her bows. Captain Wilkes of the U.S. man-of-war *San Jacinto* sent a rowboat to take off Mason and Slidell and their secretaries, leaving their indignant womenfolk to continue the voyage. Great were the rejoicings in New York when Wilkes appeared with his prisoners, and loud was the fury in Britain when the *Trent* docked without them. Wild stories went round London of how the life of Slidell's daughter had been threatened by brutal U.S. Marines. The British Prime Minister, Lord Palmerston, tended to sympathise with the Confederates anyway, and he was not the man to stand high-handed treatment from the North. The French, Austrian and Prussian Governments sent notes to Washington urging that Mason and Slidell should be released, and the British Minister there anxiously asked Lincoln what he was going to do about the case. "Oh, that'll be got along with," replied Lincoln.

The President's common sense and that of the dying Prince Consort in England combined to prevent war. The Prince softened down a harsh message from the British Government to the Federal one, and the President kept quiet until the first excitement was over. Then he let Mason and Slidell out of their comfortable Boston jail, to start their journey again on another British ship.

Later, Lincoln admitted that it had been hard to swallow his pride and give in. He had felt like a sick man who, sure he was dying, had sent for his bitterest enemy and staged a touching reconciliation, but as the visitor was leaving, almost in tears, had called after him, "See here, Brown, if I should get well, mind, that old grudge still stands!"

And, putting it another way to Seward, the President observed, "One war at a time."

Mrs Mary Lincoln

New Year, 1862 – No More Oysters on the Potomac

During the first weeks of 1862 the President was tired and discouraged. There was a great deal to worry him. Even his family life was shadowed with anxiety and grief. Mrs Lincoln had been a lively girl when he married her, but the joy went out of her when the war came. It put her in a cruel position. One of her brothers and three of her half-brothers were actually fighting for the Confederates, and the Northerners remembered this, but forgot that other members of her family were devoted Federals. She found the ladies of Washington difficult to make friends with. And then in February one of her children, an attractive little boy called Willie, fell seriously ill. Within a few days he was dead. She was distracted with grief, and became a very trying companion. Lincoln's secretaries could not bear her. Lincoln himself was the most loving of fathers and the kindest of husbands, and her sufferings added enormously to his own.

At the same time the war was going badly. True, the Federals had an ever-growing army, a new rifled gun that could shoot farther and more accurately than anything the Confederates could lay hands on, and a tightening stranglehold on the Confederate seaports. Yet somehow they were winning no victories.

Lack of first-class commanders was part of the trouble. McClellan, who had seemed such an excellent choice, was not justifying the country's hopes. Besides, McClellan was ill over the New Year. It was said that he had typhoid fever, and Lincoln was not even allowed to see him. "The bottom is out of the tub," said the harassed President to one of his generals. "What shall I do?"

He seriously thought of taking direct command himself. Years ago he had studied law and turned himself out a professional lawyer. Now he studied military manuals, and if he didn't turn himself out a professional soldier, he did learn a great deal about soldiering. He acquired a good grasp of overall military situations, and could judge how to distribute his armies, and where to apply pressure, better than any of the Union generals who had yet become prominent. For the next two years, he played an important part in the actual conduct of the war.

As the months passed there came some gleams of comfort. For one thing, the soldiers were no longer shoddily equipped, because he was able to get rid of Cameron. It was part of Cameron's duty to draw up reports to Congress, and in one of these he included a passage saying that slaves should be freed and used as soldiers in the Federal armies, as a punishment to "rebellious traitors" who owned them. Lincoln ordered this passage suppressed, but it reached the newspapers, and so did the order for its suppression. Everybody was angry – the slaveowners in the

North because Cameron had made his remarks, the anti-slave enthusiasts because Lincoln had suppressed them. That was vexatious. Still, it gave Lincoln his opportunity. He needed to send a new American Minister to Russia, and he appointed Cameron. No accusations and no incivilities were called for, and one exasperating subordinate was out of the way.

There had to be a new Secretary for War, and Lincoln chose Edward McMasters Stanton. Stanton was energetic, honest, and a bit of a bully. He had been in the habit of calling Lincoln "the original gorilla" or "the Illinois Ape", but that did not matter to Lincoln – if Stanton was the right man for the post, Stanton should have it. Once in office, Stanton worked devotedly and soon learned to respect his admittedly long-armed and hairy chief. However, he did not always obey him in small matters, and Lincoln knew this and was good-humoured about it. When his orders and Stanton's conflicted, he would say cheerfully, "Did Stanton tell you I was a damned fool? Then I expect I must be one, for he is almost always right, and generally means what he says."

Stanton undoubtedly meant what he said when he observed, "This army has got to fight or run away. . . . The champagne and oysters on the Potomac must be stopped." And when an officer was slow in obeying an order to send guns to Harper's Ferry, Stanton himself turned out and helped load them onto railway trucks. Next day the officer apologetically said he was about to see to it. Stanton rapped out, "The guns are now at Harper's Ferry, and you, sir, are no longer in the service of the United States Government."

Spring, 1862 – Movement on the Mississippi

In the western theatre of war the Confederates held the Mississippi River as far north as the borders of Kentucky and Illinois, where the Ohio flows into it and the Cumberland and Tennessee flow into the Ohio. These waterways were very important to them, for they had few railways and often sent men and supplies by boat. The Confederate general who commanded in this area was Albert Sidney Johnston. The local Federal forces outnumbered his, but left him almost in peace for most of the winter. In February he saw that the Federals were stirring. Queer armoured craft were slipping down the Mississippi from the north. He retreated

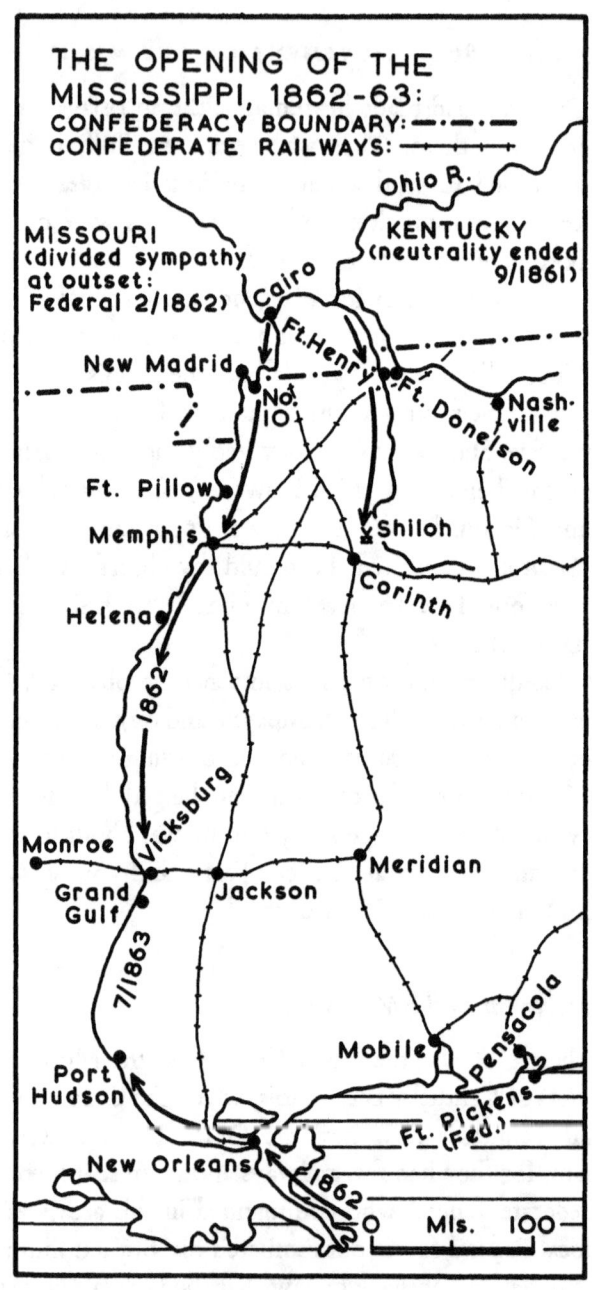

Map II

a little and prepared to block that river at Island Number 10, near New Madrid, and the Cumberland and the Tennessee at Fort Donelson and Fort Henry respectively. The Federals, he knew, were likely to attack any or all of these points. He asked Jefferson Davis for reinforcements: but the Confederates were short of men, and no reinforcements came.

On February 6th his fears were realised. The Federal General Ulysses Grant seized Fort Henry, and its garrison escaped to Fort Donelson. Ten days later Fort Donelson, too, was taken. Grant was not yet well known or much trusted, but he was really the most determined of the high-ranking officers on the Federal side. When the Confederates at Fort Donelson asked for terms, he replied, "No terms except an unconditional and immediate surrender." There was a hard battle, which left Grant victorious, with both forts, sixty Confederate guns, and fourteen thousand Confederate prisoners. He did not follow up his success at once, because he was not the senior officer in that area, and his superior, Halleck, was no hustler. It was some weeks before Halleck ordered him to combine with Buell and attack Johnston at a place called Corinth.

Johnston did not wait to be attacked: he chose to take the initiative and strike at Grant before Buell could join him. It was at Shiloh, a few miles north of Corinth, that he caught Grant on the march. Grant fought stubbornly, knowing that Buell was on the way to him, but he was only just able to hold out. Most of the day went by before the first of Buell's men arrived. Next morning the position altered: Confederates were mown down by Federal Artillery or put to flight, and Johnston himself was fatally wounded.

The North was not so much elated at the victory of Shiloh as appalled at its cost. Over thirteen thousand Federal soldiers were wounded, missing or killed. Hard things were said about Grant – that he had allowed himself to be taken by surprise, that he had sacrificed men through incompetence, that he had been drunk on the battlefield, and that he should be dismissed from his command. Grant himself was miserable. He seriously thought of resigning, and his friend Sherman went into his tent and spent some strenuous hours talking him out of it. But the last word was with Lincoln: "I can't spare this man – he fights."

Immediately after the battle of Shiloh, Fort Number 10, the last of the Confederates' river-fortresses in that region, was taken by General Pope. Corinth itself fell to the Federals in June. Yet more important, the Federal Admiral Farragut, with cool daring, ran a squadron of gunboats past the forts that guarded the mouth of the Mississippi and landed soldiers in New Orleans. The Confederates burned cotton, provisions, gunboats – anything that might be useful to the Federals – and abandoned the city.

There was still a stretch of river in Confederate hands, from Memphis to New Orleans. However, Farragut was able to demonstrate that the Confederates could not keep this stretch clear of Federal gunboats, if the gunboats were handled with skill and courage. Apart from that, the movement on the Mississippi died down for a time, because the Federal armies were now concentrating on the eastern theatre of war.

March to April, 1862 – The "Merrimac" and the "Monitor"

Back in Washington, McClellan recovered from his illness, but let the weeks go by without making a move. Lincoln wanted him to go straight for Richmond, but he put forward a plan of his own which sounded as good or better. If his men were shipped down Chesapeake Bay to Fort Monroe – a Federal stronghold – they could be landed on the peninsula between the James and the York Rivers, and would have a comparatively short march overland to Richmond, which they could then tackle from the east instead of from the north. This plan was approved. McClellan asked for 150,000 men. Lincoln consulted other generals, and decided that he could not spare so many. He must reserve 35,000 to 40,000, under the command of McDowell, to protect Washington. Over 100,000 would still be left for McClellan, but McClellan did not think it enough. He even ordered McDowell to join him, but Lincoln circumvented that order and McDowell stayed behind.

Lincoln could see that for the time being there would be no room in McClellan's head for anything but his own campaign, which, indeed, would be enough to keep any man busy. Accordingly he relieved him of his post as Commander-in-Chief and left him with only his own force, the Army of the Potomac, to worry about. This was necessary, but perhaps it was natural that McClellan did not like it. Nor did he take kindly to Lincoln's suggestion that he should act fast and break the enemy's lines at once. He wrote to his wife, "I was much tempted to reply that he had better come and do it himself."

Then came a hitch. Lying at Norfolk, across the river from Fort Monroe, the Confederates had an extraordinary-looking vessel called the *Merrimac*. She had once been a frigate of the U.S. Navy, and the Federals had scuttled her near the coast. The resourceful Confederates had salvaged her, built an iron superstructure to close in her decks and provided her with ten seven-inch guns. Her prow was reinforced with metal so thick that she could ram almost anything. Weighed down in this way, she could only just move through the water – but no gunfire could hurt her. On March 8th, out she lurched from Norfolk, and engaged some Federal ships that were blockading the river mouth. She rammed and sank one, and then turned and smashed a second. A third was only saved by running aground; the *Merrimac* could not float in shallow waters. News of this incident came to Washington as an unpleasant shock. If the Federals could no longer control the mouth of the James River, it would be risky for McClellan's troops to land.

Welles, the Secretary of the Navy, said that only one Federal ship was capable of standing up to the *Merrimac* – namely, the much smaller *Monitor*, which had been designed by the famous Scandinavian Ericsson and only just completed. She, too, was encased in iron. Her decks were almost flush with the water, and she had an ungainly look, as someone said, "like a cheesebox on a raft". The cheesebox part was a revolving turret with two guns. Rough seas might sink her – and they nearly did, as she made her way down the coasts – but no enemy fire could do so.

Stanton looked dubious, but it was agreed to send the *Monitor* into action. The *Merrimac* was still at large. The two ships approached each other, clashed, and drew away, neither of them seriously damaged. The *Monitor* fired and hit the *Merrimac* with a shock that made the crew's noses bleed: the *Merrimac* fired, and the captain of the *Monitor* was temporarily blinded. So it went on for some hours. At last the *Merrimac* put into Norfolk again, and the *Monitor* was ordered to stand by.

Nothing now prevented the landing of McClellan's troops, and in early April great numbers were put ashore. But it was May before the *Merrimac* was finally disposed of. Lincoln was then visiting McClellan, and was disturbed to find that nothing more had been done to remove the menace. He ordered the Federal gunboats to attack Norfolk. Out came the *Merrimac*, but at sight of the *Monitor* she turned back into port. The gunboats had things pretty well their own way. One shore battery was wrecked, then a second; and when the Federal troops landed there was very little resistance. The Confederates blew up their military supplies before abandoning the town. One large explosion announced that the *Merrimac* had gone. So perished the first of the ironclads. She helped to make history in more ways than one, for naval authorities all over the world now realised that their vessels were out of date, and took to armour-plating as a necessary protection.

McClellan on the Peninsula

Meanwhile McClellan's army, having disembarked at Fort Monroe, moved very cautiously inland. There was no hope of keeping its movements secret. The Confederates could see perfectly well what it was up to: the only question was, could they stop it? They withdrew to Yorktown, and brought down from Manassas General Joseph E. Johnston – no relation of the Albert S. Johnston who was killed at Shiloh.

Most historians think that Johnston did not mean to sacrifice too many men on defending Yorktown and would have given it up fairly readily in the face of a really determined assault. McClellan thought otherwise. As usual, he fancied that he was up against overwhelming strength, and he spent weeks in preparing to besiege Yorktown, all the time imploring Lincoln to let him have the troops left under McDowell to protect Washington. He complained of having only 85,000, and Lincoln, who was aware of having provided him with about 108,000, wondered what had happened to the rest. He said that sending men to McClellan was like shovelling fleas across a barnyard: you never knew how many would arrive.

In the first week of May, McClellan was satisfied at last that his preparations were complete. He advanced to Yorktown, only to find that the Confederates had quietly taken themselves off and that his elaborate work was practically wasted. However, the fall of Yorktown opened the York River to Federal ships, and as it was at this point that Norfolk, too, was taken, the Federals could count on plenty

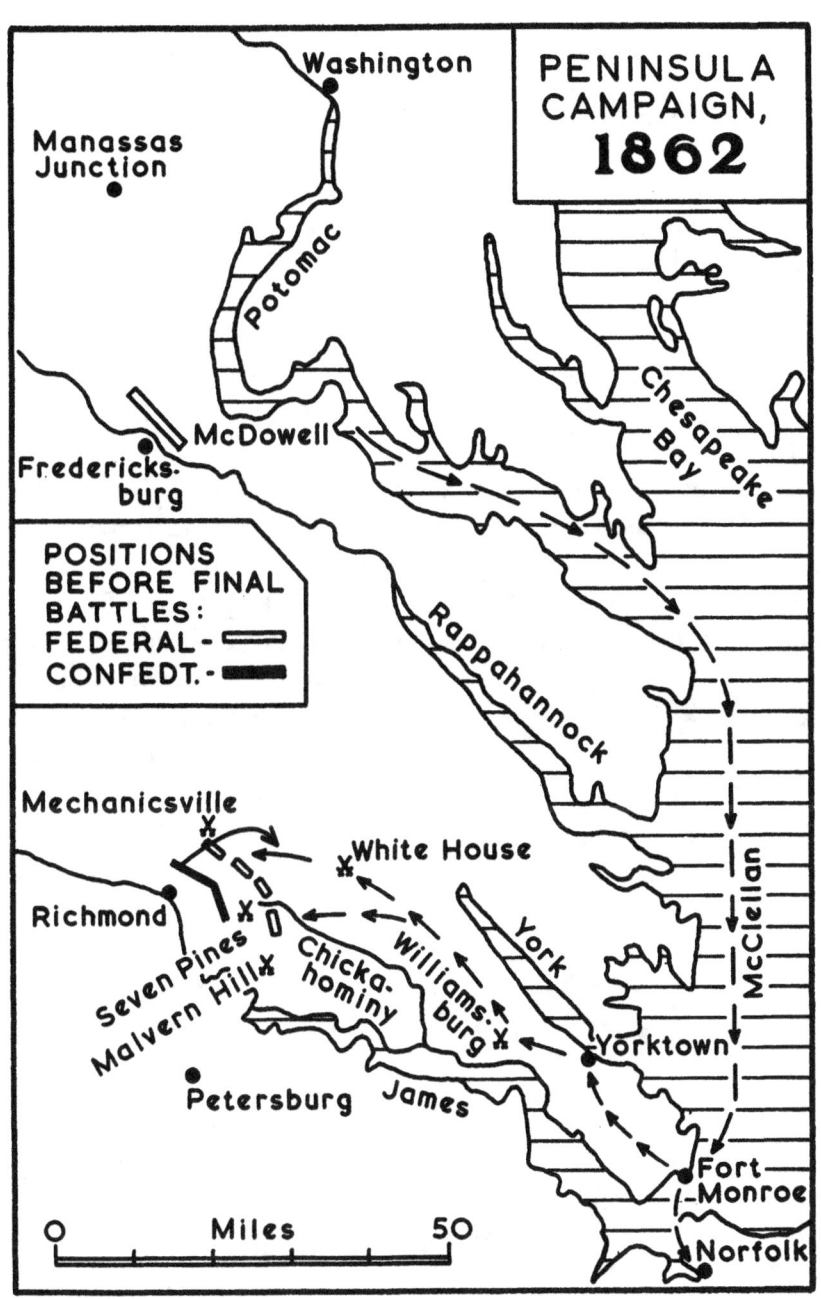

Map III

of backing from gunboats on both sides of the Peninsula. McClellan could go forward.

He caught up a section of the Confederate army at Williamsburg and did it a great deal of damage. Then he pressed on to White House. Sixty miles or so were behind him: he had some twenty-five to go before reaching Richmond. The big moment was coming. Once again he appealed for those extra men, and Lincoln was inclined now to let him have them. It would be worth taking a risk, for the fall of Richmond might well mean the end of the war.

But the Confederates had been given precious time and they knew how to use it. They had, in the Shenandoah valley, one of their ablest generals – "Stonewall" Jackson. Jackson's men had earned the nickname for him by their steadiness at Bull Run. He now showed that he was as good at flinging them round the country as he was at making them stand fast. He had only about 16,000, but with them he fought a brilliant campaign along the Shenandoah, keeping four Federal generals guessing for about a month. At length two of these, Shields and McDowell, combined and chased him up the river. He drew them on for some distance and then turned and gave battle, and defeated them both. The news of defeats at Cross Keys and Fort Republic, on June 8th and 9th, made Lincoln change his mind about sending McDowell to McClellan's aid. Nobody knew where Jackson would appear next – and it would be disastrous if he swooped down on Washington and found it poorly guarded.

In point of fact, Jackson went in a different direction. Moving at prodigious speed, he made for Richmond, to help in its defence.

Then it rained. The little Chickahominy River rose so high that it

Stonewall Jackson

could not be crossed, and McClellan's men were on both sides of it. His army was split in two. Johnston was not strong enough to tackle it all at once, but he could and did engage the weaker section in battle. There was fierce fighting at Seven Pines in which he himself was wounded. This and more rain brought McClellan up short. He was within five miles or so of Richmond now, but the land was waterlogged – and McDowell's 35,000, who might have strengthened his right flank, were still withheld from him.

At the same time Jefferson Davis ordered General Lee to take over from the wounded Joseph Johnston. This was a disadvantage for the Federals, because, though Johnston was a fine soldier, Lee was a finer one. Among other things, Lee made excellent use of his cavalry as scouts. He sent a dashing young officer, J. E. B. Stuart, with twelve hundred horsemen to investigate McClellan's right wing. Stuart did more than was expected. Having got the required information and found that it would be very difficult to return the way he had come, he rode right round McClellan's army and back to Richmond, where he presented his reports and several hundred prisoners. This was one of the most spectacular feats of the war.

Lee now knew exactly how McClellan's men were placed and how many were still cut off by the Chickahominy River. His own army was smaller than McClellan's, but might smash it by applying pressure in the right place at the right moment. He planned a circular movement to take McClellan's right wing by storm and then swing round and catch the main force in the rear. This would leave only 16,000 men between McClellan and Richmond, and if McClellan advanced quickly enough he might be in the town before the circular movement was complete. But advancing quickly was not McClellan's strong point, and Lee knew it.

The plan did not work out quite as he had hoped. The first part – the assault on McClellan's right wing – was successful. It was this right wing that was cut off from the main body by the swollen river. General Porter, who commanded it, was taken by surprise at Mechanicsville. He fought stubbornly, but was driven back, and would probably have been overwhelmed if Jackson had joined the Confederates just then as had been expected. But the heavy rain which so bothered the Federals hindered the Confederates, too, and Jackson was delayed. There were seven days of bitter fighting, and several thousand Federals were taken prisoner, twenty Federal guns captured. At last, McClellan's right wing was broken up and his communications with White House destroyed, and he was almost surrounded.

He made up his mind in the nick of time to escape from Lee's closing circle. He would go south, to the James River, where fresh supplies could reach him from the sea. With much difficulty and many losses he fought his way to Malvern Hill, a strong position on the river bank: and there he withstood a furious attack. The Battle of the Seven Days ended with the hurling back of the Confederates, and with Federal gunboats adding their cannonade to the fire of the weary Federal Army.

Lee's manoeuvre had lost him over 20,000 valuable men and the chance to cripple the Federal Army for good. But it had saved Richmond. McClellan was willing to try again, but Lincoln ordered him to bring his men back north to Aquia Creek by sea.

The failure of the Peninsula campaign was not entirely McClellan's fault. He had moved too slowly and shown too little dash, but he might have succeeded if he had had the reinforcements he had begged for – or even if the weather had been kinder. He had assured Lincoln that the Peninsula was good, firm marching ground. He had been wrong there – but people often *are* wrong about prospects of rain. And he had fought vailiantly in a long, desperate battle. Not all the criticism levelled at him by the politicians seems to have been justified.

However that may be, Lincoln did not restore him to the overall command of the Federal Armies. Instead he appointed General Halleck, a man with plenty of textbook knowledge but little initiative and little gift for leadership. The soldiers called Halleck "Old Brains". They did not mean it as a compliment.

The Army of Virginia was handed over to a showy, self-confident officer called Pope. Pope boastfully declared that his headquarters would be in the saddle. This remark prompted Jackson, who seldom joked, to declare that he was not much afraid of a man who did not know his headquarters from his hindquarters.

August, 1862 – Second Battle of Bull Run

While McClellan's army was being shipped north from the James River the Confederates could not afford to rest and lick their wounds. The short respite was too precious to waste. Jackson, with 24,000 men, hurried off to Gordonsville, Virginia, to harass General Pope. He had some success, but not as much as he hoped, because

AUGUST, 1862 – SECOND BATTLE OF BULL RUN

Pope got wind of his plans. Something more effectual must be done quickly before the whole of McClellan's army could take the field again.

About fifty miles north-east of Gordonsville lay Manassas Junction. Johnston had had to abandon it in order to defend Richmond from McClellan, and it was now in Federal hands. It was a key point, not only because of the railways but because the Federals used it as a depot for supplies of food, guns and ammunition. The Confederates were badly in need of these things. To capture Manassas would be well worth while.

Jackson was the obvious man for the task, and Lee sent him off with about 20,000 men by a circuitous route through the hills, with orders to cut the Alexandria-Orange railway and fall on Manassas from the west. Meanwhile the main Confederate Army quietly moved up in support. Pope did not realise what was going on until a terrific conflagration at Manassas told the whole countryside that Jackson had reached it, sacked it, and set it alight. By the time Pope was on the scene there was nothing left of it but ashes. Jackson's men had helped themselves freely to everything (except drink, on which the officers had set a guard) and then melted away into the mountains.

Pope had something like 70,000 troops and more were pouring ashore at Aquia Creek. He was ready to tackle Jackson – if he could find him. Jackson kept him guessing for a day or two, so as to give the main Confederate force, under Lee and Longstreet, time to approach. On August 30th, however, he emerged into the open. At Bull Run there was an epic struggle, and for the whole of that day Jackson's 20,000 were pitted against 53,000 Federals. When evening came he said, "They have done their worst."

On the 31st both sides were reinforced. General Porter, who had had such a bad time on the Peninsula, came to Pope's aid and had if anything a worse time still. He was engaging Jackson when the main Confederate force came bursting out from the woods and fell upon him, forcing him to retreat. He was afterwards court-martialled and deprived of his command, a piece of injustice which was reversed some years later at another trial. Pope's position was not nearly so desperate. Numerically he was still strong, but he had no hold over his officers, many of whom openly resented having been transferred to his command from McClellan's: he lost heart and retired to Washington.

This second battle of Bull Run was more disastrous to the Union than the first. The Confederates had taken the initiative: they could not now be prevented from overrunning Maryland: they might even take Washington. Foreign powers, including Britain, were thinking of recognising their Government and of offering to mediate between them and the Union. Lincoln and Halleck were in despair. Pope had failed them badly, and in their extremity they turned again to McClellan.

There have been varied accounts of McClellan's behaviour in this crisis. He himself had no objection to slavery: he mistrusted the politicians of the Union: he was bitter because his troops had been taken from him. It is said that he purposely delayed sending reinforcements to Pope, and he advised Lincoln to let Pope "get out of his scrape" as best he could. But now, when Lincoln appealed to him to save Washington, he undertook to do it. He rode to meet the retreating army, which gave him an almost hysterical welcome. Soldiers crowded round to kiss his horse's legs. His spirits rose: he set to work, and in a few weeks he had the men in fighting order again.

September, 1862 – Antietam

Lee did not, in fact, try to take Washington as the Federals had feared. He had not the necessary strength. However, he had hopes of prising loose the Federals' uncertain grip on Maryland. In the first weeks of September he and Jackson were known to be at large to the north and west of Washington, but their exact movements could be foreseen only by a most extraordinary chance. A Federal soldier casually picked up three cigars wrapped in a scrap of paper – and on the paper were notes of Lee's immediate plans.

That was how McClellan learned that Jackson was about to take Harper's Ferry, while Lee was making for Hagerstown, farther north, Jackson was to join him there and move on with him to Harrisburg, in Pennsylvania. Thus the Confederate force would be divided for a time, and, if McClellan could catch it while scattered, he might destroy the fragments.

He did, in fact, intercept Lee at Turner's Gap, and do him enough damage to force him back without disabling him completely. After that he hesitated. It was the same old story: he was really twice as strong as the enemy, but thought himself

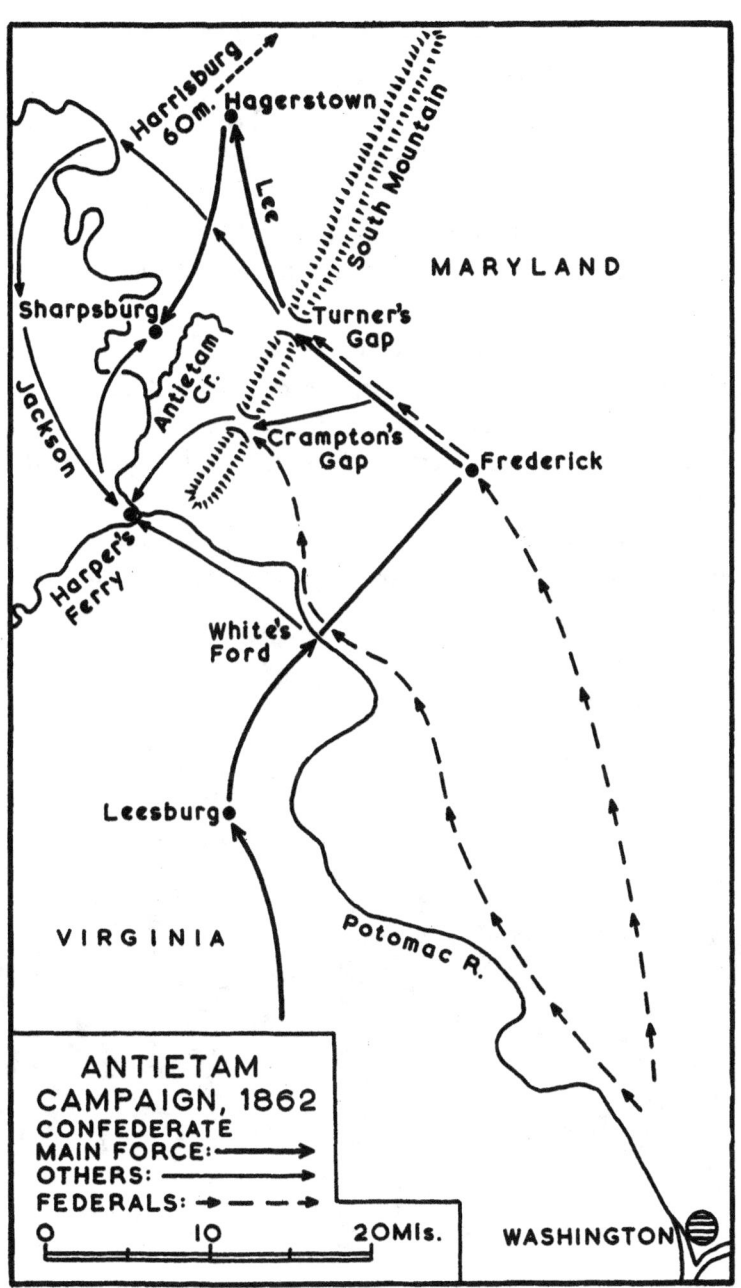

Map IV

only half as strong. Then he reckoned, correctly, that his cavalry was not nearly as good as Lee's. He could not depend upon it, as Lee could on his, to bring in accurate reports. So he acted with his customary deliberation and Lee with his customary speed. And Jackson duly took Harper's Ferry, left his officers picking up vast stocks of rifles and ammunition, and hastened to Lee's support. They were together when McClellan confronted them on the banks of the Antietam, a small tributary of the Potomac River.

Nevertheless, they were outnumbered in the battle of the Antietam by two to one. They had the Potomac at their backs, as McClellan had had the James at his back at the end of the Peninsula campaign, but for them there were no friendly gunboats blazing away in their defence. One narrow bridge offered the only possible escape.

They fought all day on September 17th, and by nightfall had lost 13,000 men. Most of the officers were in favour of retreating over the bridge, but Lee decided to

Lincoln visiting McClellan and his officers on the battlefield of Antietam

stand his ground until next morning. He expected McClellan to attack again. So did Lincoln, who telegraphed anxiously, "Please do not let him get off without being hurt." But nothing happened. McClellan did not attack, and Lee, who wanted to, was persuaded not to by his officers. On the 19th he began to cross the river into Virginia and comparative safety.

Lincoln could hardly believe that McClellan would not follow him up at once. It was a chance in a million. But McClellan dallied for five whole weeks. He made excuses, saying among other things that his horses were footsore. Pope, in disgrace because of his blunders at Bull Run, commented sourly that with McClellan in command victory was more dangerous to the Union than defeat. Nobody knew what to make of it, least of all Lincoln, who began to wonder whether McClellan really wanted to hurt the enemy. The fact that McClellan was not an anti-slavery man gave a handle to the many disgusted politicians who wanted him out of the way. At length Lincoln yielded to their pressure and to his own conviction that the war could never be won like this. At the beginning of November he relieved McClellan of his command – this time for good.

The Emancipation of the Southern Slaves

Lincoln had much besides the actual fighting to occupy his mind. Foreign relations were a constant worry. In the eyes of Europe, the North's cause was a good one, for Europe disapproved of slavery, which the South was fighting to preserve. Yet Europe was enormously impressed by the courage and resourcefulness of the South in the face of such heavy odds. Admiration threatened to overcome moral sentiment. Gladstone, the British Chancellor of the Exchequer, said, "We may have our own opinions about slavery, we may be for or against the South, but there is no doubt that Jefferson Davis and the other leaders of the South have made an Army: they are making, it appears, a Navy: and they have made what is more than either, they have made a Nation."

It was necessary, therefore, to stress the slavery issue for Europe's benefit: to appeal strongly to anti-slavery feeling, especially in England. The Union would win the support of the English working classes, if not of the English Government, if it were to abolish slavery in the South.

For some time past many people in Washington and throughout the Union had been urging Lincoln to do this. Charles Sumner and Thaddeus Stevens were among them, and there had been deputations from various religious sects and articles in the *New York Tribune* to the same effect. Lincoln himself wanted to do it, if it could be done without violating the Constitution. He had begun to think it could. The Confederate States were fighting against the Union and could not expect the Union to protect their rights. What was not justified in peacetime might well be justified in war. Lincoln did get a Bill through Congress to free the slaves of the District of Columbia. Several times during 1862 he tried to persuade the border States, Kentucky, Maryland, Missouri and Delaware, to pass similar Bills, on the understanding that slaveowners would be compensated. But the border States remained unmoved. Since they were loyal, nothing could be done without their consent, but the rebel States were another matter. In July the President called a Cabinet meeting and read out a draft proclamation freeing all slaves in the Confederacy. The Cabinet considered it, and Seward said that it might be a good thing, but only if issued at the proper time. During defeats was not the proper time. The Proclamation would seem then like a desperate resource – an appeal to the Negroes to help kill white men. Lincoln saw the point. He put the proclamation aside. In September, after Antietam, he judged that the moment had come to publish it. He gave warning that on January 1st, 1863, he would declare that slaves in the rebel States were free immediately and for ever. Missouri, Kentucky, Maryland and Delaware would be unaffected: so would any other State that had joined the Union and was fairly represented in Congress by the given date.

The response among the Negro population was jubilant, but elsewhere it was disappointing. In England, though the working classes sent encouraging messages, the nation as a whole could not understand why Lincoln did not make a clean sweep of slavery altogether. In the Union, abolitionists wanted to know what was the use of the President's declaring slaves free in the areas not under his control, while in some of the areas that *were* under his control slaves were still in bondage. The Democrats, many of whom approved of slavery and resented any suggestion that they had gone to war to suppress it, fumed openly. There grew up an active party of "Copperheads" – called after a poisonous kind of snake – who wanted the

Lincoln reads the Emancipation Proclamation to his Cabinet

war brought to an end at once, whether slavery went on or not. There were many desertions from the Army and not enough new volunteers.

When the New Year came Lincoln kept his promise, and became a hero to those Negroes who understood what he had done. It is not easy to judge how the slaves in the South were affected at the time. Many went on working on the plantations, often directed by the planters' wives in the planters' absence. Some of these did not know anything about the Proclamation. Others escaped to the Federal lines and applied to join the Federal Armies. Lincoln was unwilling to send them into the firing-line, because he was afraid that they would be mercilessly treated by the Confederates if they were captured, and he preferred to set them to work as non-combatants. But a lot of them were not content with that. They wanted to share with white men the danger and dignity of active service. As time went on whole regiments were formed of Negro soldiers, and the 54th Massachusetts – to mention only one of these – distinguished itself in battle.

Between the warning in September and the Proclamation on January 1st there were Congressional elections, which went to show how the nation as a whole felt about Emancipation. The reaction was unfavourable: the Republicans lost many seats. The Presidency was not directly affected by these elections – Lincoln's term had two years still to go – but they were a sign that discontent was in the air.

December, 1862 – Fredericksburg

McClellan's successor was General Burnside, a pleasant, energetic man, but one who rightly thought himself unfit for such an exacting post. He accepted it, not through ambition, but because there was nobody else to take it.

Burnside wanted to march straight on Richmond from the north, via Fredericksburg. He consulted Lincoln about this plan, and Lincoln approved of it provided it was to be carried out at once. Delay would give Lee time to recover and might be disastrous. But, as so often happened with the Federals, there *was* delay. The way to Fredericksburg was barred by the Rappahannock River running just north of it, and to cross this Burnside needed pontoon bridges. They were not ready for a fortnight. Meanwhile Lee – rather against his own judgement, for he would have preferred to meet Burnside farther south – devoted himself at Jefferson Davis's order to the building of walls, trenches and gun emplacements on the high ground behind Fredericksburg town. From these he could command an open plain which sloped down to the river.

Just before Burnside's assault Lincoln visited him and strongly advised him to distract the Confederates' attention and draw off some of their men by feint attacks across fords farther up the river, to the west. Burnside did not take this advice. Perhaps he felt that sheer weight of numbers would carry him through, for he had about 118,000 to Lee's 80,000. But the 118,000 were exposed to deadly fire as they crossed the river on the pontoons and charged up the slope beyond, while Lee's 80,000 were comparatively snug in their prepared positions. Nearly 13,000 Federals fell, and less than half that number of Confederates. Burnside's officers and men, ready to take sane risks, shrank from being massacred. When the day was over and Burnside wanted to prepare another assault they objected. Lincoln thought them justified. He forbade Burnside to try again.

After this disaster, many people pressed advice on the President. Burnside, for one, declared that he would resign unless Lincoln dismissed Halleck. Lincoln, not satisfied with either man, decided to keep Halleck and let Burnside go to a less important command. That meant finding yet another general to take over in the east. At the same time, there was an agitation among the Senators to get rid of Seward, the Secretary of State, whom Lincoln could not spare; and he knew that behind this agitation was Chase, who was almost as valuable. He contrived not to lose either of them. He got letters of resignation from them both and accepted neither. The governmental machine was creaking badly: he had to oil the works and, somehow, keep it going.

So another year ended in disappointments, defeats and recriminations. But Lincoln was far from giving up. On the contrary, he had still to get into his stride.

Early 1863 – Chancellorsville

In January, Lincoln appointed Hooker to succeed Burnside, and there was a three-month lull while Hooker reorganised his infantry and built up a new cavalry corps, ten thousand strong. By April he had what he called "the finest army on the planet". He intended to use the whole of it to destroy Lee in one great battle. Lee, he knew, was at Chancellorsville, a few miles south of the Rappahannock and a few miles west of Fredericksburg. He would send two corps under General Sedgwick to cross the river at Fredericksburg and attack Lee's army from the east, while he himself, with three more corps, forded it some miles upstream and moved in from the west. Meanwhile the new cavalry under Stoneman would harass Lee in the rear – that is, from the south.

His movements were well known to Lee, who again used that superb cavalry-man, J. E. B. Stuart, as an intelligence officer. But it looked doubtful whether Lee's foreknowledge could save him. Fine generalship on his part and Jackson's, perfect co-operation between them, and the skill and daring of the Southern cavalry, were all needed to pull him through.

Stoneman's horses were held up for a while by floods, but on April 30th they crossed the river and were able to work round to the south of Lee's army as planned, and threaten Lee's communications with Richmond. But Stoneman was

Robert E. Lee

no match for Stuart. He was outmanoeuvred so cleverly that when the battle started in earnest he was not in a position to take part in it, whereas Stuart could throw himself into it at a decisive moment.

Meanwhile Lee and Jackson decided that Jackson, with 25,000 men, should slip out from the closing circle of Federal troops by some little-known road, and then smash that circle from the outside. A suitable road was found, and all seemed to be well and the Federals unaware of what was happening, when a Federal general caught sight of Jackson's rearguard and attacked and dispersed it. Strangely enough, this turned out to be luckier for the Confederates than for the Federals. For the Federals imagined that the main Confederate Army was in flight, and Hooker was filled with false confidence. On the evening of May 2nd the 11th Corps of the Federal Army was placidly having supper and looking forward to victory on the morrow when Jackson's 25,000 burst upon it from the woodlands in its rear. An hour's fighting and it was reduced to a shambles.

Night came. Jackson fell a victim to his own daring and the alertness of his own men. He saw a chance to reconnoitre the Federal lines of communication, and, with only a small group of officers, rode off into the darkness. It was characteristic of him to work fast without telling many people of his intentions. He was coming back when some soldiers from Carolina saw him move, took him for the enemy, and fired. His wounds were so serious that he was unconscious before he could give an account of his raid.

When they knew that he had been wounded his devoted men, shouting his name, hurled themselves at the Federal lines and fought their way through to rejoin Lee on the far side. Stuart, who took them over, fought splendidly.

The Federals were now in confusion. To add to their difficulties, they were in wild, wooded country where it was extremely hard to tell what was going on. Hooker seems to have been demoralised, but a slight head wound stunned him for a time and saved him from being held altogether responsible for disaster. It certainly was disaster. Sedgwick, who fought on bravely, could not do much to retrieve it. The Federals had started with twice as many men as the Confederates. They lost 5,000 more than the Confederates did, and those that were left, sadly battered, struggled back into safety across the Rappahannock.

It was a week before Jackson died. He did not seem to realise that his case was

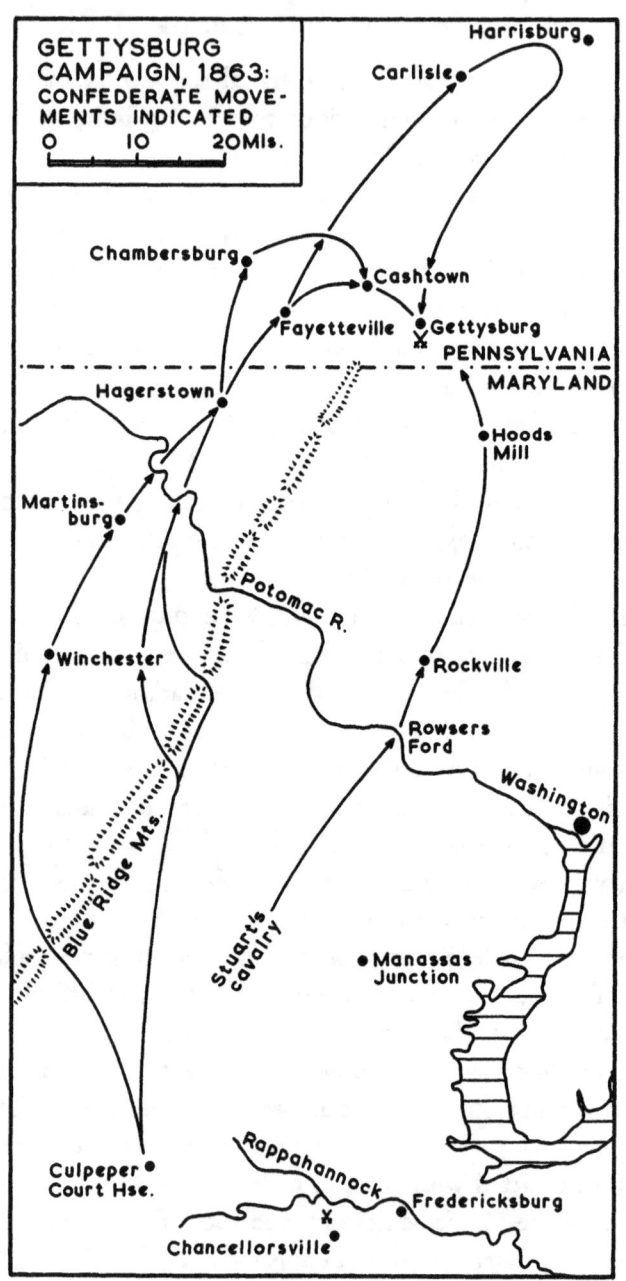

Map V

hopeless: when they told him so, he looked surprised and said, "Very good, very good; it is all right."

"Such an executive officer," said Lee, "the sun never shone on."

The losses of Chancellorsville had to be made up. So far the Northerners had relied on volunteers: now they introduced conscription. Each town had to send its quota of men, and if enough did not come forward the rest had to be found by drawing lots. A man whose name was drawn might still avoid service by paying a substitute. There was much grumbling and many towns were hard put to it to make up their quota, so that most of them offered sums of money – "bounties", as they were called – to each volunteer. It was common for men to "jump the bounty" by enlisting, deserting, and re-enlisting over and over again, collecting the money each time.

July, 1863 – Gettysburg

Lee wanted to follow up his success at Chancellorsville by invading Pennsylvania. He felt that a spectacular victory there was the only thing that could win the war for the Confederates; besides, he was more than ever in need of the supplies that could be found only in Northern territory.

He divided his army into three parts, commanded respectively by Generals Longstreet, Hill and Ewell, and all three moved northwards. Everything went well with them at first. Ewell cleared the Federal troops out of Winchester and Martinsburg, took Hagerstown, and advanced to within four miles of Harrisburg. Lee, with Hill and Longstreet, was approaching the same point by a different route, through Chambersburg. As usual he depended on Stuart to keep him informed of the movements of the Federals. But for once Stuart miscalculated, and, to avoid being caught and slaughtered by Hooker's main army, he had to make a long detour which meant that he lost contact with Lee for a whole week. The consequences of this were serious.

Meanwhile, Richmond had been left almost unprotected. Hooker thought this was a good chance of seizing it, but Lincoln insisted that it was more important to defeat Lee and the Confederate Army. As a matter of fact, Lincoln had lost confidence in Hooker, and when Hooker offered his resignation Lincoln moved him to a lesser command and put General George Meade in his place. Meade prepared to carry out Lincoln's policy of finding the main Confederate Army and giving battle.

He supposed that Lee would make for Baltimore, and planned to meet him twenty miles or so to the north-east of that town. As a matter of fact, Lee did not want a pitched battle just at that moment. He turned north, intending to concentrate his troops at Cashtown.

On June 30th a brigade of Hill's corps chanced to be in Gettysburg – to look for shoes rather than for any other purpose. (There were times when the Confederate armies were so ill-shod that it was said that they could be traced by the bloodstains left on the roads by the feet of their marching soldiers.) There they found Federal cavalry already in possession. The Federal commander thought it a good place to make a stand – for it was an important road junction – and summoned reinforcements to the spot. This forced the Confederates' hand. Ewell came down from the north-east, and drove the Federals southwards, to an eminence known as Cemetery Ridge. Both sides rushed all available men to the scene. The battle of Gettysburg was on.

Lee wanted to storm Cemetery Ridge, but his commanders demurred. Longstreet, in particular, argued in favour of an outflanking movement. This might have been effective if Stuart had been there with his cavalry, but Stuart had not yet appeared. Eventually Lee ordered Longstreet to attack Meade's left wing at dawn on the following day (July 2nd). Longstreet delayed many hours: the Federals, meanwhile, were reinforced: and the Confederate attack was badly co-ordinated. Lee must have felt the need of Jackson very acutely.

As a result Meade was able to hold his own, though his losses were terrible. On the afternoon of July 3rd, the third day of the battle, a Confederate division of infantry under Pickett made a magnificent charge. Up the slope of Cemetery Ridge it marched, flags flying, while the Federal troops on the crest watched and held their fire. Then, when the range shortened to about a thousand yards, the Federal guns whined and thundered. The Confederates' ranks showed gaps, closed up again, and came on. One general reached the Federal guns with a hundred of his men about him, before he was shot down. The Federal position was stormed – but the Confederates could not hold it. They had no reserves. They had to fall back,

Confederate soldiers captured at Gettysburg

stepping over the bodies of those who had fallen during the advance. Two-thirds of Pickett's division, and two of his generals, were left dead on the slopes.

Next day both armies were exhausted. Lee's began to trail away to the south, and Meade's did not pursue it. The Potomac, swollen with rain, lay across Lee's line of retreat: if Meade had been on his tail he might have been forced to stand again and suffer yet more slaughter. As it was, Meade allowed him a week's respite, and by July 14th his army was across the river.

Meade was satisfied that he had done his duty in "driving the invader from our soil", but Lincoln was bitterly disappointed. "Will our generals never get that idea out of their heads?" he said. "The whole country is our soil." Again, as after Antietam, Lee seemed to be at the Federals' mercy – only to slip out of their grasp. All the same, Lincoln expressed his appreciation of Meade's skill and bravery and the victory he had won.

Gettysburg was indeed an important victory – the turning-point, historians say, of the whole war. The Southerners had lost about 29,000 men. They could not afford to go on at that rate. Brave as they were, they were being bled white. There were no more battles in the eastern theatre of war for the rest of that year.

Nowadays Gettysburg is world famous, less for the battle fought there than for the speech Lincoln made that November when he opened a ceremony for the soldiers who had been killed. Lincoln, in that very speech, prophesied that the opposite would be true. This is what he said:

Fourscore and seven years ago, our fathers brought forth upon this continent a new nation, conceived in liberty and dedicated to the proposition that all men are created equal.

Now we are engaged in a great civil war, testing whether that nation – or any nation so conceived and so dedicated – can long endure.

We are met on a great battle-field of that war. We are met to dedicate a portion of it as the final resting-place of those who have given their lives that that nation might live.

It is altogether fitting and proper that we should do this.

But, in a larger sense, we cannot dedicate, we cannot consecrate, we cannot

Lincoln delivering the Gettysburg Address – from a painting by Fletcher C. Ransom

hallow, this ground. The brave men, living and dead, who struggled here, have consecrated it, far above our power to add or to detract.

The world will little note nor long remember what we say here: but it can never forget what they did here.

It is for us, the living, rather, to be dedicated, here, to the unfinished work that they have thus far so nobly carried on. It is rather for us to be here dedicated to the great task remaining before us; that from these honoured dead we take increased devotion to that cause for which they here gave the last full measure of devotion; that we here highly resolve that these dead shall not have died in vain; that the nation shall, under God, have a new birth of freedom, and that government of the people, by the people, for the people, shall not perish from the earth.

1863 – The Western Theatre

For the best part of a year Grant had been trying to find a way of taking Vicksburg. The town was perched high above the Mississippi River and protected on its landward sides by malarial swamps and almost impenetrable forests. It was stoutly defended by the Confederate General Pemberton, who vowed that he would not give it up until the last scrap of food had gone and the last man had perished. And it was highly important. Across the river it commanded Arkansas, and Louisiana could send much-needed supplies to the other Confederate States which had born the brunt of the fighting. If Vicksburg fell and the Federals controlled the whole river, the Confederacy would be cut clean through. Besides, a key railway ran through the town, linking Monroe in Louisiana with the town of Jackson in Mississippi and the railroad system of the South-West.

Twice Grant tried to storm Vicksburg and failed. He set troops to work with spades and shovels, trying to wreck its communications. He marched and manoeuvred in the swamps and forests, and sometimes Washington had no news of him for a week or more. Politicians said he was unfit for his job, repeated old stories about his drunkenness, and clamoured for his recall. "I think," said Lincoln, "Grant has hardly a friend left except myself" (he might have added, "and Sherman"). But he also remarked that if he knew what kind of whisky Grant drank, he would send a barrel or so of it to some other generals. He had never met Grant, but he was aware of his quality.

In the summer of 1863 Grant justified Lincoln's faith. He alarmed and bewildered Pemberton by feint attacks on Vicksburg from the north, meanwhile marching his troops down the far bank of the Mississipi, ferrying them across the river, and assembling them at Grand Gulf, some thirty miles to the south. Pemberton, in his anxiety, called for reinforcements, and General Joseph Johnston set out to bring them, though he had scarcely recovered from his wounds. They did not arrive, for Grant was now in a good position to intercept them and drive them back. Pemberton rashly attempted to cut Grant off from his base at Grand Gulf, but Grant was not really worried about Grand Gulf: what he wanted was a chance to get at Pemberton. And by emerging from his fortifications Pemberton had given him that chance. There was a fierce battle at Champion Hill, and Pemberton was defeated with heavy losses before retiring to Vicksburg again.

For the third time Grant tried and failed to carry the fortress by assault. There was nothing left to do but to starve Pemberton out. The Federals settled down to a siege which lasted through the second half of May and all June. On July 4th, the last day of Gettysburg, Pemberton had to surrender. In his bitterness he behaved rather insolently to Grant, but Grant, however merciless in battle, was never vindictive when the battle was over. He ordered food for Pemberton's starving men, and boasted that their feelings were not hurt by anything said or done by his own.

At about the same time the town of Jackson fell to General Sherman, and a few days later Port Hudson, the last Confederate stronghold on the Mississippi, also capitulated. Good news poured into Washington from the West. Lincoln hugged Welles and joyfully remarked, "The Father of Waters again goes unvexed to the sea."

Autumn in Tennessee

Grant's reputation was made. In October, Lincoln gave him command of the departments of the Ohio, Cumberland and Tennessee Rivers, while Sherman, under him, was put in charge of the Army of Tennessee.

Their next task was to save the situation at Chattanooga. This town on the banks of the Tennessee River was important, because it was a junction from which railways radiated to all parts of the South. The Federal General Rosecrans had been sent in September to take it from the Confederate General Bragg. Rosecrans had been cautious while the fate of Vicksburg was still in doubt. His infantry had raided Confederate ironworks, while Confederate cavalry had attacked his communications; beyond that there had been little fighting. But when Vicksburg fell Rosecrans became more active. He moved on Chattanooga with skill and confidence, and took it from Bragg, mostly by manoeuvre.

He then reckoned mistakenly that Bragg's army was beaten. It was really still full of fight, and was lurking in the nearby mountains, gathering strength. Presently it was reinforced by five brigades under Longstreet – a somewhat slow and deliberate officer, but not one to be disregarded. Rosecrans, unaware of this, dispersed his men widely. He realised his danger too late, and had only just concentrated them again and was still at a disadvantage when Bragg pounced.

There was a desperate battle at Chickamauga, with the Confederates getting the best of it. Sixteen thousand Federal soldiers were lost, and forty guns. Only one Federal corps came through without being driven in disorder from the field. Its commander, George E. Thomas, was nicknamed the Rock of Chickamauga.

Rosecrans's situation was then desperate. He was almost surrounded by Confederates, who held the mountain-tops overlooking the area. The Tennessee River, which he used as a supply line, was blocked. Halleck was very slow in sending help. Eventually there arrived a corps under Hooker, and later still, in November, came Grant and Sherman.

Hooker cleared the Tennessee River and proceeded to take one of Bragg's mountain strong-points. His "Battle above the Clouds" won him lasting fame, and half obliterated the painful memory of Chancellorsville. Sherman cleared the Confederates from another mountain-top. But there remained a third, which fell to Thomas, the Rock of Chickamauga. Acting, it seems, without orders, and to the utter surprise of the enemy, he suddenly had his troops charging up the slopes, cleared two lines of entrenchments and established himself on the crest. Grant pressed him his advantage, and sent the Confederates retreating in disorder southwards.

So ended 1863 and all hope of victory for the Southerners. They had failed in their Pennsylvania campaign, they had lost the whole length of the Mississippi and nearly all Tennessee. The only thing that still kept them going was grim determination not to stop.

Justice or Mercy?

It was in October, 1863, that Rosecrans suggested to Lincoln that, now the war was going better, it might be wise to offer a general amnesty to officers and soldiers who had taken part in the rebellion. Lincoln had had some such thing in mind. In December he added to his annual message to Congress a Proclamation, guaranteeing pardon to all rebels except for a few leaders, provided they would take an oath of loyalty to the Constitution and would swear to support the Government's policy of Negro emancipation.

It would have been utterly unlike Lincoln to plan revenge or punishments. Indeed, punishments were a constant vexation to him. He realised that they were necessary – for keeping the Army in order was difficult enough – but it was open to him to spare any particular offender, and he was always being tempted to do it. A brigadier-general claimed that one reason for the Army's failures was that its deserters were too often pardoned by the President, whereas the Confederates shot theirs. He added that there was no need for Lincoln to interfere with punishments at all, since Congress took the responsibility. "Yes," said Lincoln, "Congress has taken the responsibility, and left the women to howl after *me*." On another occasion he declared, "If I should go shooting men by scores for desertion, I should have such a hullabaloo about my ears as I have not heard yet, and I should deserve it. You cannot order men shot by dozens or twenties. People won't stand it, and they ought not to stand it."

Sherman admitted that he himself often had deserters shot before Lincoln had the chance to pardon them. This was irregular, but it is said that other generals, including Grant and Thomas, did the same.

Nevertheless, Sherman was grateful to Lincoln for upholding authority, in a somewhat unorthodox way, at what might have been an awkward moment. Sherman was then only a colonel. A soldier complained to Lincoln that he was due to be released and that Sherman had threatened to shoot him if he tried to go. Lincoln looked from the soldier to Sherman and from Sherman to the soldier, and solemnly said that if he were in the soldier's shoes he would be very careful, as Sherman looked to him like a man of his word.

Another time, when frantically appealed to on behalf of a condemned man, he slowly remarked that he didn't think shooting would do the man much good, and signed an order for his reprieve.

He was particularly merciful in cases of young soldiers found asleep on sentry duty. At least one youth who had been rescued by Lincoln from a disgraceful death went on to distinguish himself in battle and die very differently, grateful to the last.

Once a terrified fourteen-year-old was brought to him, half expecting to be shot. He had run away to enlist while under age. Lincoln reached for some paper and scribbled a note to Stanton: "Hadn't we better spank this drummer-boy and send him back home . . .?"

Unhappy New Year, 1864

January and February, 1864, went by with very little fighting. Jefferson Davis's hold on the Confederacy was weakening: politically, he had not much control: but in military matters his was the last word, and he would not let his generals take the initiative. Even now Lee and Longstreet were ready with plans for an offensive, but they were talked down. Lee was told to concentrate on defending Richmond.

Lincoln's position as head of the winning side was almost as unpleasant for a man of his kindly nature. He had to go on hitting an enemy that was really defeated but would not give in. He knew that the South would not accept his terms while it had any strength left. It would not be enough now to re-establish the Union on the old basis, half slave, half free. He had declared the Southern slaves liberated and had admitted them to the Army. He could not go back on that.

There were rumours that the Confederates were suing for peace. Lincoln denied it, but with his usual tolerance he allowed private citizens to go through the lines and talk to Jefferson Davis for themselves. Davis seems to have received several of them quite cordially, and to have had frank,

Jefferson Davis

interesting conversations. It was friendly and civilised – remarkably so when one remembers the slaughter that had been going on – but it lead nowhere. The peacemakers came back admitting that Lincoln was right.

Later in the year, the lively editor of the *New York Tribune*, Horace Greeley, wrote to the President telling him that two ambassadors from the Confederacy had arrived in Niagara, ready to treat. Lincoln took this with a pinch of salt. He declined to go chasing off to Niagara himself, but asked Greeley to go, and to bring back anyone who turned out to be an official emissary of the South. He added that it was useless to suggest any terms short of the return of the South to the Union *and* the abolition of slavery. Greeley went – but, as Lincoln expected, the men turned out to have no authority at all. Nevertheless, Greeley pleaded with Lincoln to let them know that he *would* receive them, if Jefferson Davis liked to make them his accredited agents. Lincoln refused. The sufferings of the South distressed him beyond words – but it was for the South, not for the Union, to ask for peace. Greeley was still not silenced. He criticised the President in his newspaper, and held him responsible for the fact that the war went on. Lincoln put up with it: he thought it would not be good for the war effort to show up an influential man like Greeley as a pacifist; rather than that he would let his own reputation suffer.

Meanwhile the weary business of killing Confederates must be carried on. At least he now had a commander who was fit for it. In March he invited Grant to Washington, and gave him the rank of Lieutenant-General and authority over all the United States Armies. Grant, sturdy, inelegant and unassuming, was out of place in the great reception-rooms of the White House, where a crowd of notables pressed forward to get a glimpse of him and he was obliged to stand on a sofa and stutter a few embarrassed words. Lincoln came to his rescue and they talked in private. They had not met before, but they liked and understood each other at once. Before Grant left, Lincoln wrote assuring him that he would not ask for details of his plans, but would back him to the limit. "While I am very anxious that any great disaster or capture of our men in great numbers should be avoided, I know that these points are less likely to escape your attention than they would mine. If there is anything which is within my power to give, do not fail to let me know it. And now, with a brave army and a just cause, may God sustain you." In his reply Grant said that he had always been generously supplied with what he wanted, and that he had never even been pressed for explanations. "Should my success be less than I desire, the fault is not with you."

Sherman, in the West, was hoping that Grant would go back there, even though that would stand in the way of his promotion. But Grant reckoned that Sherman could manage alone, and appointed him to the high command of his area, where he would be able to make use of General Thomas – a soldier whom Sherman had always admired and trusted, and who had now taken over Rosecrans's post.

Meade would probably have more important work to do than Sherman would, and was less fitted for it. Grant kept him at the head of the Army of the Potomac, but intended to keep a close watch on him, and give him any guidance needed. As a matter of fact, Meade hardly ever had to act entirely on his own initiative, from that time on.

Each of the two generals had a Confederate commander to mark. Meade was to follow every move of Lee's, Sherman every move of Joseph Johnston's.

May, 1864 – Grant in the Wilderness

Grant's first campaign in the eastern theatre was fought over old battlegrounds – the region of Fredericksburg, where Burnside had come to grief, and Chancellorsville, where Hooker had been outmanoeuvred. It was known as the Wilderness. Rough country, overgrown with trees and scrub, it could swallow up an army as a cornfield swallows up rabbits. Somewhere in its midst Lee would be keeping watch. Grant hoped to catch him in a trap by an outflanking movement, and smash him.

He couldn't do it. Again and again he was held up by a frontal attack that he would have preferred to avoid: again and again he tried to work eastwards, round Lee's right wing: again and again Lee forestalled him. This was the kind of fighting that suited the Confederates better than it suited the Federals. Superior numbers and superior weapons counted for less than knowledge of the country, good scouts and quickness to seize an advantage. Both sides suffered acutely, but the Federals' sufferings were the worse. Every now and then fires broke out, and wounded soldiers, unable to save themselves, cried out for help lest they should be burned alive.

General Ulysses Grant with officers

After two days of this horror (May 5th and 6th), Grant pressed on into the rather more open neighbourhood of Spotsylvania and made for a railway junction close by. But Lee got there first. By the time Grant's troops arrived Lee's had chosen the best positions and dug themselves in. Both sides fought savagely and the battle raged for over a week. Grant was still unable to work round Lee's right or to penetrate his defences. All day long Federal ships were steaming up the coast with loads of wounded men to be disembarked in Washington. Now hospitals had to be improvised in the capital and hearses and ambulances filled its streets. But Grant had declared his intention of going on with the campaign, even if it took the whole summer.

Once more he shifted ground, moving southwards in the hope that Lee would attack his leading corps and be taken in the rear by the rest of the Federal Army, or else would make a stand on open ground where sheer numbers might overwhelm him. But Lee moved quickly and warily, like a goalkeeper protecting his goal. He slipped across a couple of rivers and drew up his men in a new, semi-circular position, still covering Richmond.

June – Cold Harbor

Grant came to the conclusion that Lee could not be outmanoeuvred, but must be crushed by brute force. He sent General Sheridan ahead with the cavalry and some light infantry to take Cold Harbor, a village about five miles north-east of Richmond, which would serve as a base. He himself followed with the main force. Lee forestalled this move, too, interposing his troops between Grant's and Richmond along a six-mile front. His line was nowhere strong. Someone asked him what reserves he had to bring up in case it should be broken, and he replied, "Not a regiment, and that has been my position since the fighting commenced. If I shorten my lines to provide a reserve, he will turn them: if I weaken my lines to provide a reserve, he will break through."

Grant was intent now, not on turning the line but upon breaking it. On June 3rd he sent his whole army into the attack. Lee's resisted heroically. About 7,000 Federals were hit within an hour or so, and lay, dead or dying, before the Confederate trenches. The rest were driven back and refused to try again. Firing went on for ten days between the two armies, facing each other across a hundred yards or so of ground. After the third day, Lee offered a short truce, so that the bodies might be taken up and carried away to hospitals or to graves. Grant accepted. Then the bloody business started once more.

The Confederate line would not break, and Grant again had to abandon his plan as hopeless. He would go yet farther south, and from that direction he would batter his way into Richmond over the bodies of Lee's men, or else he would starve them into submission by means of a siege. It was a grim prospect either way, and there was no telling what it would cost in lives and in time.

Autumn, 1864 – Grant at Petersburg

It was two years since McClellan had crossed the Peninsula from north to south, fighting furiously as he went. Grant was able to do the same with hardly any opposition. Lee was now too weak to think of anything more than to keep him out of the Confederate capital.

There had been all this while a Federal army on the James River, commanded by General Butler, and Grant had already ordered Butler to attack Petersburg, a town more than twenty miles to the south of Richmond, which was an outpost of defence. Butler had bungled the job. Grant now tried himself, with the aid of a huge mine which Burnside was to explode. Somehow or other Burnside bungled, too. Petersburg could not be taken by storm, and Grant had to besiege it. The siege lasted throughout the autumn, while people in Washington grumbled about the delay and the appalling expenditure of men. Lincoln himself was unhappy, but he still trusted Grant. Here at least was a general who could not be suspected of reluctance to hurt the enemy. Besides, Grant, as Commander-in-Chief, was not forgetting the other theatres of war, and from these at any rate good news was coming in.

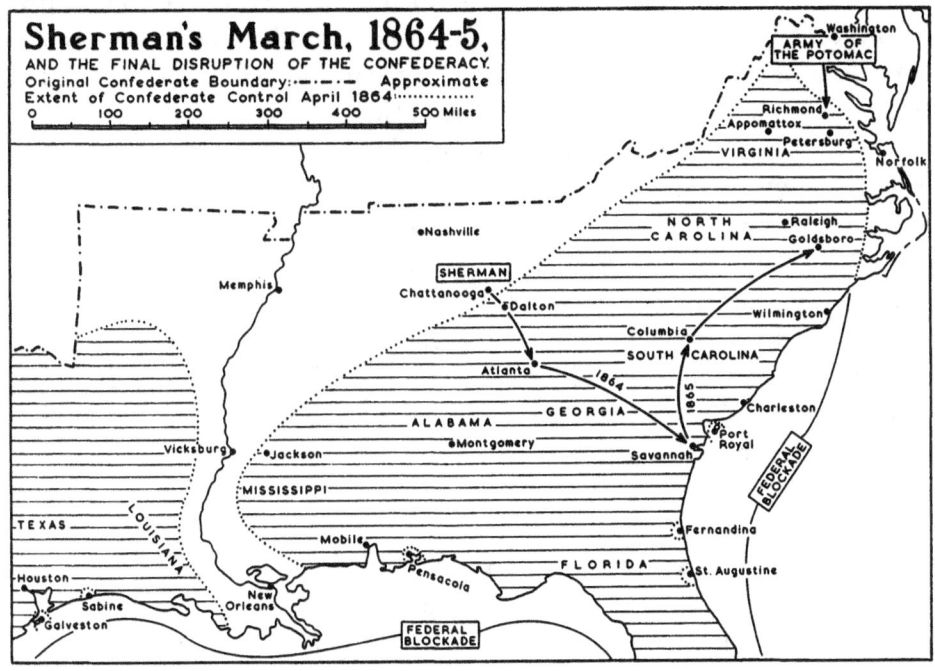

Map VI

Summer, 1864 – Sherman's March Through Georgia

It is necessary now to go back some months, to the day when Grant moved south across the Rappidan to fight the battle of the Wilderness. On that day Sherman, too, moved south from Chattanooga. He was making for Atlanta, a hundred miles away in Georgia. His plan of action was rather like Grant's – to move slowly, avoiding pitched battles if he could, trying to work round the enemy's flank.

His opponent was Joseph Johnston, an excellent defensive fighter, who was not in favour of unnecessary bloodshed. Johnston fell back and back before him, from one entrenched position to another, delaying and harassing him, but not inviting him to open battle. Only once did Sherman try to storm Johnston's trenches, and then he was repulsed.

Johnston's policy was probably the right one, but Jefferson Davis lost patience with it. In July he replaced him by General Hood. Hood was fierce, but ineffectual. Sherman defeated him in three battles, and moved into Atlanta on September 2nd.

His lines of communication were now very long and very vulnerable, and he decided not to bother about them. He warned Grant that for some time he would be no more heard of. He proposed to plunge right into enemy country, and march, as the song puts it, "from Atlanta to the sea". So as not to have the furious Hood buzzing in his immediate rear, he asked Thomas to take care of him, drawing him northwards if possible and silencing him when there was an opportunity.

Thomas justified his confidence. He bided his time, tempting Hood into small, wasteful attacks, letting him suffer the full discomforts of the first days of winter. Then, in mid-December, he fell on him with overwhelming force and smashed him. Sherman and his sixty thousand men were able to proceed on their march almost unhindered.

It was, as it was meant to be, a journey of destruction. Along a sixty-mile-wide track no usable railways were left, no bridges, hardly any cattle or poultry or corn. The men were told to take what food they could find and destroy all public property, but not to steal or smash private possessions or injure any civilians. By and large they followed orders. There was certainly some plundering of houses, but there were hardly any crimes of violence.

THE "ALABAMA" AND MOBILE – TWO TRIUMPHS FOR THE NAVY 69

They reached the Atlantic coast just before Christmas. Sherman wired to Lincoln that he was offering him the town of Savannah as a Christmas gift. He helped himself to the guns he found there, and turned north, through South Carolina, which he treated much as he had treated Georgia – a little more severely, perhaps. His soldiers felt a grudge against the people of South Carolina and were more difficult to control here. They took the whole thing as a triumphal progress. But Sherman himself was not blind to the reality of what he was doing. "War," he said, "is hell."

General Sherman

The "Alabama" and Mobile – Two Triumphs for the Navy

Sherman's was not the only Federal achievement of the year. There were two, major triumphs for the Federal Navy. The first was the sinking of the Confederate warship, the *Alabama*, off Cherbourg in June. The *Alabama*, and some other craft used by the Confederates, had been built in a British shipyard, and though she had never docked in any Confederate port she had done a good deal of damage to Federal ships on the high seas. Her sinking, by the *Kearsarge*, was hailed with joy in the North. After the war the United States claimed heavy damages from the British Government, on the grounds that Britain, being neutral, should not have allowed a belligerent to buy from her any vessel that was obviously designed for war. An arbitration committee ruled that Britain should pay £3,000,000 – a sum which American history calls moderate, and English history calls pretty stiff.

The second triumph was the capture by Admiral Farragut of the harbour fortifications at Mobile, on the Gulf of Mexico, in August. Mobile was one of the few seaports that was still in Confederate hands. The town itself was left to the Confederates, but its usefulness was gone, since Confederate shipping could no longer put in there. By this time, as a matter of fact, the thing was not of tremendous practical importance because the Confederates had little importing or exporting to do anyway. But the psychological effect on both sides was another matter. August was not a good month for the Northerners, who, though standing on the verge of victory, did not seem able to take another step. The news of Mobile heartened them. It silenced some of the grumblers, and rallied public opinion to the President.

Sheridan in the Shenandoah – A Triumph for the Cavalry

Much more decisive than either the sinking of the *Alabama* or the seizing of fortifications at Mobile was the successful campaign in the Shenandoah valley of General Philip H. Sheridan. It put an end to a recurrent danger to Washington, and it also put an end to the life of one of the South's most brilliant officers, J. E. B. Stuart.

While Grant was grappling with Lee, the Confederate General Early carried out two raids, one into the Washington area and the other into Pennsylvania. The Washington one was alarming. A fort that protected the town was seriously threatened. Lincoln hurried there in person, probably very glad of a chance to see some action at close quarters instead of having to worry about it from a distance. He was careless of his personal safety, and a junior officer unceremoniously bawled him out, not realising who he was. Presently he was persuaded to withdraw out of harm's way. Early was then driven off and made to retreat to the Shenandoah valley. But it was considered disgraceful that he had been allowed to come so near the capital. When he staged his second raid, the one into Pennsylvania, Lincoln was very much perturbed. He called for new recruits, but what the situation really needed was leaders; Lincoln did not want to interfere with military matters at this stage, and Halleck was never much good in a crisis. It was left to Grant to deal with the menace. He came up from the South and ordered Sheridan to the Shenandoah valley, to clear it, not only of Confederate troops, but of food supplies as well, so that no Confederate forces could use it as a base again. All this Sheridan did with devastating thoroughness. He defeated Early in a series of minor battles and one major one at Cedar Creek, and before the winter came he had laid the valley waste.

Sheridan was one of the very few first-class cavalry officers that the North produced. In this campaign he showed daring and resource. He has been much blamed for his ruthless destruction of the countryside – and indeed it left a great many civilians practically starving – but he hastened the end of the war, and that, after all, was an act of mercy.

Elections

The Presidential elections were due in November, 1864. With the country in a state of civil war, the complications were endless. Many large areas of the South had been subdued and put under Federal governors – Tennessee, for instance, was administered by Andrew Johnson, a strong Unionist. Even in the States that were still actively at war there were pockets of Unionism. Were such places to be allowed representatives in Congress? How were such representatives to be chosen, and once they were chosen would Congress accept them? It could not be forced to. Lincoln's own wish was that any State that would and could elect Congressmen by fair means should be encouraged to do so, but he and the members of his party were not all agreed as to how this should be done, and he went so far as to suppress one Bill, introduced by the more fiery Republicans, and passed by Congress as a whole. The Republicans were his own party, and many of them resented his action: but he thought that the Bill was unconstitutional and unnecessarily hard on the South. Such things affected his personal popularity and his chances of being re-elected in November. He was perfectly willing to see his place taken by any man fit to take it. The question was, where could such a man be found?

His Secretary of the Treasury, Salmon Chase, was sure that there was one good answer; in the Treasury! In some ways Chase would have made a good candidate. He was a man of high principles, and he had carried out his duties very efficiently, even though he had often made himself rather unpleasant. He now thought himself indispensable, and could not understand why the nation did not rise as one man and nominate him. He offered Lincoln his resignation, and Lincoln accepted it. That left him free to devote himself to electioneering. He circulated endless stories of grievances against Lincoln. But he was not as popular as he had fancied: the movement in his favour died down and presently he dropped out of the running.

Then there was talk of nominating Grant. Lincoln was dismayed by this, because the war had still to be won, and Grant seemed the only man capable of winning it. He sent a mutual friend to sound Grant on the subject and find out his own views. Grant's reaction was prompt and decisive. He wouldn't stand. "They can't do it," he declared; "they can't compel me to do it."

"Have you said this to the President?" asked the friend.

"No. I have not thought it worth while . . . I consider it as important for the cause that he should be elected as that the army should be successful in the field."

So Grant was out of it, but there remained McClellan. McClellan, of course, would not be deserting any military post: he was out of the Army now. Everybody knew that he had no particular objection to slavery, and the Democrats, many of whom had been pressing for peace, thought him likely to end the war on terms acceptable to the South. At the Democratic Convention in Chicago it was declared that the war had been a failure and should be stopped, and it was decided to nominate McClellan as Democratic candidate. McClellan said he objected to the resolution that the war was a failure – but he did not object to the nomination.

In June, at Baltimore, the Republicans held *their* Convention. The war news just then was good, a fact that told in Lincoln's favour. The Convention almost unanimously adopted him as candidate, and at the same time asked for a Constitutional Amendment to abolish slavery in all States. Andrew Johnson, the Governor of Tennessee, was nominated Vice-President.

Between June and November the spirits of the North went up and down. If the election had been held in August, the month of stalemate, McClellan might have won. But then the cheering news came in of Sherman in Georgia, and Thomas at Nashville, and Sheridan in the Shenandoah valley. The North conquered the dreary, insidious feeling that the war was not worth-while. Even Chase, to his honour, gave up criticising Lincoln and went round making speeches in his favour. November came – over 4,000,000 citizens voted: McClellan got 1,800,000 votes, and Lincoln 2,216,000. Lincoln was in again.

When he made his inaugural address, in March, 1865, he soberly reviewed the

The second inauguration of President Lincoln, Washington

causes of the war. He added that both sides read the same Bible and prayed to the same God. "It may seem strange that any men should dare to ask a just God's assistance in wringing their bread from the sweat of other men's faces; but let us judge not, that we be not judged. The prayers of both could not be answered –

that of neither has been answered fully. The Almighty has His own purposes." He ended with the famous words; "With malice towards none; with charity for all; with firmness in the right, as God gives us to see the right, let us strive on to finish the work we are in; to bind up the nation's wounds, to care for him who shall have borne the battle, and for his widow, and his orphan – to do all which may achieve and cherish a just and lasting peace among ourselves, and with all nations."

1865 – The End of Slavery

At its Convention in Baltimore the Republican Party had called for a Constitutional Amendment to abolish slavery. Amending the Constitution is a lengthy business. Two-thirds of each House – the Senate and the House of Representatives – must vote in favour, and then the Amendment must be ratified by three-quarters of the States in their own Legislative Assemblies. By the end of January 1865, Arkansas, Louisiana, Maryland and Missouri had already abolished slavery on their own account, so that the second part of the process – the ratification part – was sure to be carried through, but it would take some time. In point of fact it took the best part of a year. The first part – the passage of the Bill through Congress – was completed on January 31st, but only just. The House of Representatives passed it with three votes to spare. A hundred-gun salute was fired. Next day a procession marched with music to the White House to serenade the President.

The Thirteenth Amendment made slavery illegal throughout the United States for ever. It was followed in 1868 by the Fourteenth Amendment, which did away with some of the civil disabilities of Negroes, but said nothing about the vote. It was left to the Fifteenth Amendment, in 1870, to lay down that nobody should be prevented from voting because of colour, and the question of Civil Rights for Negroes still disturbs the nation.

The Amendments did not mention compensation for slaveowners, even in the States which had been loyal to the Union. Perhaps some of them wished that they had listened to Lincoln earlier, when he had tried to persuade them to let their slaves go and accept money in exchange. Now they got nothing.

Jubilant slaves carrying copies of the Emancipation Proclamation

1865 – The End of the War

The struggle for Petersburg and Richmond went on through the winter, with Grant's army still unable to close the circle and Lee's still starving inside it. Jefferson Davis may have been misled by stories of disagreements and war-weariness in the North. He still refused to buy peace at the price of Union and Abolition.

Lincoln, of course, would not accept less. But he consented to meet Alexander Stephens, the Vice-President of the Confederacy and an old friend of his, together with two other Southern leaders, and talk things over. On February 3rd, Stephens and his companions came aboard a ship at Hampton Roads for a long, good-humoured conversation with the President. Lincoln made his terms clear. He also sketched out his idea of how the South ought to be treated when the war was over, adding that he could make no promises. It would not be in his hands alone.

The talk came to nothing, for Stephens had no authority to pledge Jefferson Davis's word. Perhaps he never knew that, soon afterwards, Lincoln tried to persuade the Senate to soften the coming blow to the South. He suggested that the Southern States should be offered four hundred million dollars in United States bonds to compensate them for the loss of their slaves – half to be handed over at once if the war ended by April 1st and the rest when the Thirteenth Amendment was finally adopted. The Cabinet, to a man, said no. It was not really surprising that not one of them was as generous-spirited as he. The North, as well as the South, had something to be bitter about. Gallantly though the South had fought

The Peacemakers. *An oil painting by George P. A. Healey. Left to right: Sherman, Grant, Lincoln and Admiral Porter*

1865 – THE END OF THE WAR

and much though it had suffered, the North had fought and suffered, too. The South had lost 258,000 men: but the North had lost 359,000.

So that particular olive branch was not offered, and the armies remained in the field and Lee and Grant at their posts. Lee's was made slightly more responsible by the fact that in February Jefferson Davis at last made him General-in-Chief of all the Southern Armies. He had long been doing the work: the main difference was in the title.

Grant waited until spring came and the roads dried and Sheridan rode south to join him. Then, on the last day of March, he launched an attack. Sheridan's troops climbed the parapets outside Petersburg, tumbled into the trenches beyond, and

Richmond from the James River

The arsenal after Richmond's surrender, 1865

fought hand-to-hand with the gaunt, ragged Confederate soldiers they found there. They took 6,000 prisoners. Next day they attacked again. On April 3rd, Lee had to withdraw his men from Petersburg.

After that Richmond was beyond saving, and there was only one line of escape – the Richmond-Danville Railway. Jefferson Davis was in church when an urgent message reached him from Lee, telling him that the Government should pack up and go at once. By late afternoon he had gone, and Grant's troops, marching into the city, found it deserted, with two great fires burning. Grant, of course, knew the way the Confederates had taken, and he also knew that they had seven trains of provisions waiting at Appomattox, on a branch of the Richmond-Danville line. If they could reach those, they might hold out for a few weeks more of pointless slaughter. He was determined to prevent that. He wrote a note and succeeded in getting it to Lee:

> The results of the last week must convince you of the hopelessness of further resistance on the part of the Army of North Virginia in this struggle. I feel that it is so, and regard it as my duty to shift from myself the responsibility of any further effusion of blood, by asking of you the surrender of that part of the Confederate States' Army known as the Army of Northern Virginia.

Jefferson Davis escaping with his Ministers five days before his capture

Lee still hesitated, but when he found that Sheridan's officers had reached Appomattox before him and captured four of the supply trains, he knew that it was the end. He arranged to meet Grant at Appomattox Court House, about five miles from the station, on April 9th. Lincoln, of course, was aware of what was happening, but he wanted Grant to have the honour of receiving Lee's surrender, so he kept away.

It was an historic occasion, and Lee dressed for it in a brand-new uniform, a beautiful sword at his side. Grant turned up in an ordinary soldier's shirt without even a tunic over it. He was never dressy at any time, and never pretentious, and he was particularly anxious not to swagger or seem overbearing before his splendid, but beaten, antagonist. Lee was much the older man, and, as Grant would readily have admitted, the finer soldier. They talked pleasantly of old times when they

The surrender of General Lee

had both fought in the Mexican war, until Lee reminded Grant that they were there to discuss terms. Thereupon Grant took a piece of paper and jotted down some sentences.

The Confederate officers were to keep their swords, but they and their men must hand over all other arms. They would be given food from the captured supply wagons. They would be released on parole when the officers had sworn, on their own and their men's behalf, never again to bear arms against the Union or break the Union's laws. Grant rather exceeded his authority in promising that on those conditions they would not be harmed, but he might well feel confident that Lincoln would not blame him for it. Lee mentioned that the artillerymen and cavalrymen owned the horses in their charge, and Grant said that they should keep them: they would need them for the spring ploughing. "That will have a very good effect," said Lee. The two men shook hands, and Lee mounted his horse and rode away.

The war was really over, though it was a fortnight before Sherman received a similar surrender from Johnston and about seven weeks before the last troops in the West gave in. On Good Friday, April 14th, the Union flag was hoisted again on Fort Sumter.

1865 – The End of the President

That same Good Friday, Lincoln and his wife went to the theatre. A big audience gathered, more to see the President than to see the play. A man was posted outside the President's box, but from varied accounts given it is difficult to be sure whether he went to sleep or left his post for a moment, or whether he simply saw no harm in letting a young actor called John Wilkes Booth pass through the door. There was a moment's scuffle and a shot. Booth leaped from the box to the stage, injuring his leg, yelled, "Sic semper tyrannis!" hurried limping to the wings and was out of the theatre, riding away, before the people round collected their wits sufficiently to stop him. In the box, Lincoln had collapsed.

He lay unconscious all night in a house near the theatre. Mrs Lincoln and others were about him. But it was Stanton who was watching him when he died. Stanton said, "Now he belongs to the ages."

The assassination – from a contemporary sketch

Booth turned out to be the leader of a small, demented gang, one of whose members tried that same night to kill Seward, but succeeded only in wounding him. Apparently Booth was proud of his own deed and expected it to make a popular hero of him. In due course he was run to earth in a country cottage. His pursuers shot him as he was trying to escape.

Those That Were Left

Sherman heard of Lincoln's death while he was arranging terms of surrender with Johnston. He was worried about the possible effects on the Southerners, and ordered that the news should be suppressed until he himself had told Johnston of

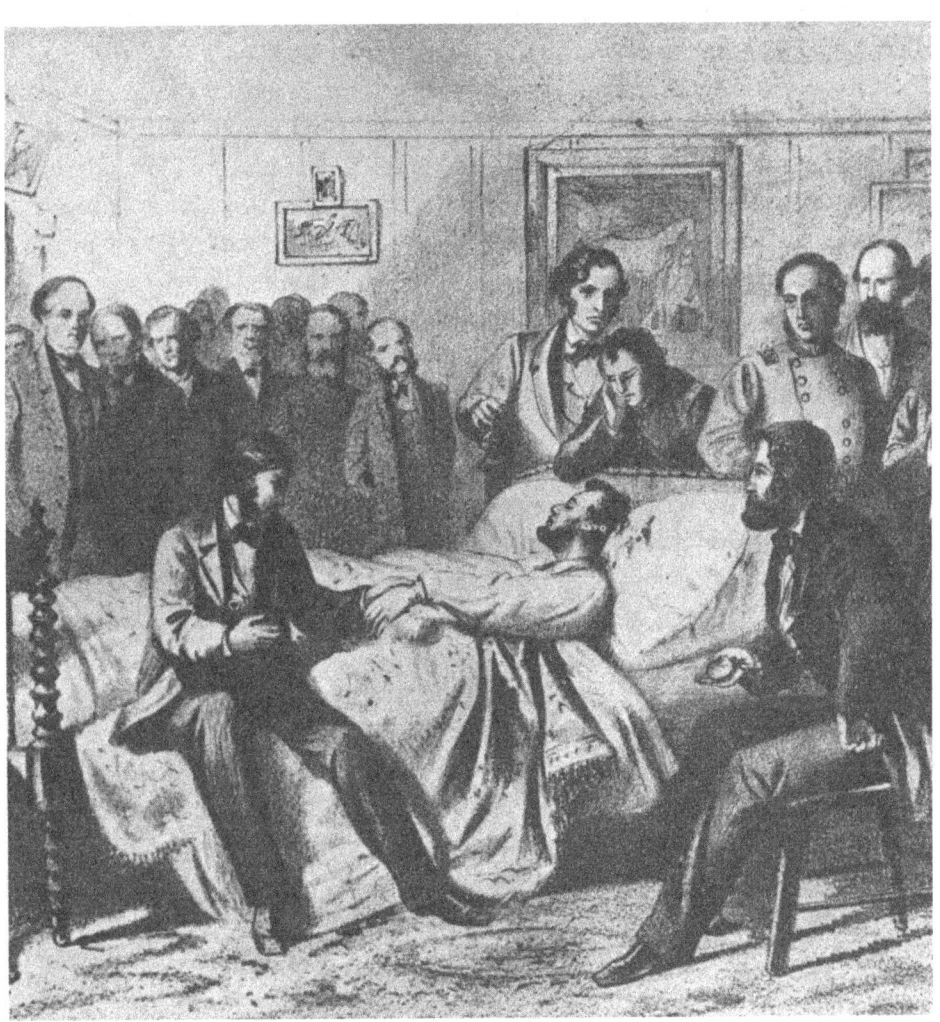

The death of Lincoln

it. When he did so Johnston broke out into a sweat, and said it was a disgrace to the age. He anxiously asked whether Sherman thought that the Confederate authorities were behind the crime. Sherman promptly assured him that nobody could dream of connecting such a thing with himself or Lee, but rather spoilt the effect by adding that he was not so sure about Jefferson Davis.

Davis was indeed suspected, quite unjustly, by some people, and there was an outcry in favour of hanging him. The Government did not go to that length. It captured him and imprisoned him for two years at Fort Monroe. His jailer even put shackles on him – but only for five days, for Stanton heard of it and angrily intervened. Eventually Davis got back his family estate, settled down there to write a book about the Confederacy, and lived to be eighty-one.

Chase's future was provided for while Lincoln was alive. When Chief Justice Taney, the old man who pronounced on the Dred Scott case, breathed his last, Chase was appointed in his stead. It was a high honour, but then, Chase was a very able lawyer.

Of the great generals, Jackson, Stuart and Albert Sidney Johnston were already dead. Joseph Johnston reached a ripe old age, published a book on military history, and became a Congressman and Government Commissioner for Railroads. Sherman still had a distinguished career ahead of him: he commanded the United States Armies for fifteen years. Thomas, the Rock of Chickamauga, was made a Major-General and in due course given his own division. Lee, the greatest of them all, did no more soldiering. He became the hard-working head of a college in Virginia, and it was noticed that he gave money freely to old soldiers, whether they had fought for the South or for the North.

Those who had wanted to see Grant President of the United States got their way in the end. But his Presidency was not very successful: it seems that he was too simple and direct in his ways to be good at detecting or preventing corruption.

The Stricken South

If ever it could be said of a political leader that his country could not afford to lose him, it could be said of Lincoln. His work might seem to be over, for the war was won and the slaves were free; but the bitterness and suffering that he had foreseen and tried to avert were infinitely the worse for his not being there.

Andrew Johnson, as Vice-President, automatically took his place and tried to carry on his policy. But the Radical Republicans who controlled Congress were

President Andrew Jackson

too strong for him. His good humour often failed when it was needed most.

He kept Lincoln's promise of an amnesty for rebels, so long as they took an oath to support the United States Constitution and thereafter observed the law. Political leaders and high-ranking officers were excepted, but they too were able to apply for individual pardons and usually got them. Each of the Confederate States was readmitted to the Union, once it had framed its own Constitution – which must give Negroes the vote – and had it approved by Congress. Meanwhile, military governors were appointed by the Federals. Most of these governors were fair-minded men.

Initiating "raw recruits" into the Ku-Klux-Klan

This does not sound harsh or unreasonable, and under the circumstances it is hard to say what else could have been done. But it meant giving votes to newly liberated and quite uneducated Negroes who, in many districts, had a greater majority than ever over the white men, since so many white men had been killed. No doubt the war itself had encouraged in these Negroes a sense of their grievances against the Southern whites. Certainly a lot of them were too simple-minded to understand that freedom from slavery did not mean freedom from work, and that now they would have to buy their board and lodging with hard cash. A rumour had spread among them that they were each to be given forty acres and a mule. They found it was only a rumour. Those who got land had to pay for it somehow – not heavily, to be sure, for it was going very cheap. Some went back to the plantations, for wages if the owners could pay any, or for a share in the crops if, as more often happened, the owners were penniless. Some did nothing at all. Thousands died of disease or starvation.

Surprisingly few, on the whole, were elected to State Conventions. But those that were had not the knowledge or experience to use their power wisely. Their first care, naturally enough, was to vote themselves enormous salaries. They could not be expected to see what most needed doing, or to know how to do it.

But there was a terrible lot to be done. The war had brought police services to a standstill, wrecked whole cities, burnt out churches and libraries, closed the schools. It had broken up railways and bridges and embankments and dams. Confederate money was worthless. Welfare workers came down from the North, with funds generously subscribed, and it was through their help that many Negroes – and many white men, too – were able to keep alive at all.

Unfortunately, other people also came from the North – the detested "carpetbaggers", who preyed on the people, buying up land for a song, selling necessities at a huge profit, worming themselves into political appointments.

In this desperate situation the former planters roused themselves and did what they could. Most had to sell their estates piece by piece or run them on the "sharecropping" system described above. Many went to work at unaccustomed jobs, and did them well. Politically, it seemed that they would be helpless in the face of the masses of Negro voters: but they refused to stand idle and watch the damage. They felt that there was only one way of saving the country from ruin and their wives and daughters from insult, and that was by terrorism. The famous "Ku Klux Klan" already existed: other secret societies of the same kind were formed, and the young men joined in great numbers. Disguised in masks and gowns, they punished unruly Negroes whom the law left untouched. They used threats and violence to keep the Negro population from voting. It is impossible to tell now how many Negroes were scared into submission, or beaten up, or even lynched, and with what justification. Far easier to point out so long after the event that such things need not have happened if the slaves had been liberated more slowly, and had been systematically prepared for freedom, and if their masters had been compensated instead of ruined. At any rate, whatever one thinks of their methods, the secret societies did help to get matters under control.

After that the work of reconstruction went fast. Six months, and a new city was springing up from the ruins of Atlanta, new bridges were spanning the rivers, and new roads and railways were being opened. A few years, and new cotton mills were being started, each with its own houses, schools and shops for workers, its own doctors, its own cemetery. New deposits of coal and iron were found, and Birmingham, Alabama, developed into one of the greatest pig-iron centres of the world. Oklahoma was opened up. New cottonfields were planted in the West. By 1870 the worst of the horror was over. The South could never go back, but it had plenty to go forward to.

ORDER OF EVENTS

1803		Purchase of Louisiana by the United States.
1809		Birth of Lincoln.
1847–49		Lincoln in Congress.
1854		Kansas-Nebraska Act.
1858		The Great Debates.
1860	November	Lincoln elected President.
	December	Secession of South Carolina.
1861	January	Secession of Alabama, Georgia, Louisiana.
	February	Secession of Texas.
	February	Confederates set up a Provisional Government.
	March	Lincoln's 1st Inauguration.
	April	Confederates take Fort Sumter.
	April	Secession of Virginia, Arkansas, North Carolina, Tennessee.
	May	General Butler (Federal) occupies Baltimore.
	July	Defection of West Virginia from Confederates.
	July	Defeat of Federals at 1st Battle of Bull Run.
	November	The *Trent* Affair.
1862	January	Stanton appointed Secretary for War.
	February	Federals seize Forts Henry and Donelson (Mississippi area).
	March	Federals seize Fort No. 10 (Mississippi area).
	April	Battle of Shiloh (Mississippi area).
	April	Battle of the *Merrimac* and the *Monitor* (Richmond area).
	April	McClellan (Federal) lands at Fort Monroe (Richmond area).
	May	McClellan occupies Yorktown.
	May-June	Battle of the Seven Pines (Richmond area).
	June	Confederate victories at Cross Keys and Fort Republic.
	June-July	Battle of the Seven Days (Richmond area).
	August	Battle of Malvern Hill (Richmond area).
	August	McClellan withdraws from the Peninsula.
	August	Jackson (Confederate) attacks Pope at Gordonsville.
	August	Federals defeated at 2nd Battle of Bull Run.
	September	Confederates take Harper's Ferry.
	September	Federal victory at Antietam.
	November	McClellan relieved of command.

ORDER OF EVENTS

	December	Federal defeat at Fredericksburg.
1863	January	Proclamation of Emancipation.
	April-May	Federal defeat at Chancellorsville.
	May	Death of Stonewall Jackson.
	June	Confederates take Winchester, Martinsburg, Hagerstown.
	June-July	Federal victory at Gettysburg.
	July	Federals take Vicksburg (Mississipi area) after long siege.
	October	Federals take Chattanooga.
	October	Federals defeated at Chickamauga.
	October	Federal victory, "Battle Above the Clouds".
	November	Gettysburg Address.
1864	March	Grant in command of Federal Armies.
	May	Battle in the Wilderness.
	May	Battle of Spotsylvania.
	June	Battle of Cold Harbor.
	June	Siege of Petersburg begins.
	June	Sinking of the *Alabama*.
	August	Federals take Mobile.
	September	Sherman (Federal) in Atlanta, Georgia.
	Sept-Oct	Sheridan (Federal) victorious in Shenandoah Valley.
	November	Lincoln re-elected President.
	December	Sherman reaches Savannah.
1865	January	Slavery abolished in Arkansas, Louisiana, Maryland, Missouri.
	January	Passage of Amendment to abolish slavery.
	February	Lincoln discusses peace terms with Stephens.
	March	Lincoln's 2nd Inauguration.
	March	Grant and Sheridan storm Petersburg.
	April	Confederates abandon Petersburg.
	April 9th	Lee surrenders to Grant at Appomatox Court House.
	April 14th	Union Flag hoisted at Fort Sumter.
	April 14th	Lincoln assassinated.
	April 26th	Johnston surrenders to Sherman.
	May	End of Confederate resistance.
	May	Capture of Jefferson Davis.

A SELECT BOOK LIST

BY NORMAN STONE, A.L.A.

AGAR, HERBERT. *Abraham Lincoln*. Collins (Makers of History Series), new edn. 1965. Illus., maps, tables. An excellent outline biography originally published in the "Brief Lives" series.

CATTON, BRUCE. *The Centennial History of the Civil War*. 3 vols. Gollancz. Vol. I, *The Coming Fury*, 1962. Vol. II, *Terrible Swift Sword*, 1963. Vol. III, not yet published. Maps, book lists. For the advanced student.

CATTON, BRUCE. *This Hallowed Ground: the story of the Union side of the Civil War*. Gollancz, 1957. Maps, book list. An account of the Civil War from the Northern point of view.

CRAVEN, AVERY. *The Coming of the Civil War*. Cambridge, 2nd edn. 1957. The causes of the Civil War.

DUPUY, R. E. and T. N. *The Compact History of the Civil War*. Prentice-Hall, 1960. Maps, book list.

HARLOW, R. W. *The United States: from wilderness to world power*. Cape, 1955. Illus., maps, book list. A standard one-volume history containing contemporary drawings.

HASKELL, FRANK A. *The Battle of Gettysburg*. Eyre & Spottiswoode, 1959. A classic eye-witness account by a Union officer who later fell at Cold Harbour.

RUSSELL, SIR WILLIAM HOWARD. *My Civil War Diary*. H. Hamilton, 1954. Illus. Sir William Russell was the famous war correspondent of *The Times*.

SANDBERG, CARL. *Abraham Lincoln*. Cape, 1955. Illus., book list. Originally published in 1937 in two volumes.

STAMPP, KENNETH M. *The Era of Reconstruction: America after the Civil War, 1865–1877*. Eyre & Spottiswoode, 1965. Book list. An account of the aftermath of the Civil War.

SIMMONS, HENRY E. *A Concise Encyclopaedia of the Civil War*. Yosseloff, 1965.

WOOD, W. B., and EDMONDS, SIR JAMES E. *The Civil War in the United States, with special reference to the campaigns of 1864 and 1865*. Methuen, reprinted 1958. Table, maps, book list. A work which has become a minor classic.

INDEX

Alabama, the, 69
Amendments to the Constitution, 74
Anderson, Major, 21
Antietam, 44
Appomatox Court House, 80
Aquia Creek, 40, 41

Ball's Bluff, 25
Booth, John Wilkes, 81
Bragg, General B., 59, 60
Brown, John, 12
Buchanan, President, 18, 20
Buell, General, 33
Bull Run, 24, 41, 42, 45
Burnside, General A. E., 48, 49, 67
Butler, General B. F., 23, 67

Cameron, 17, 18, 30, 31
Carpet-baggers, 87
Cedar Creek, 71
Cemetery Ridge, 54
Champion Hill, 59
Chancellorsville, 49–51
Chase, S. P., 17, 49, 71, 72, 84
Chattanooga, 59, 68
Chickamauga, 60
Clay, Henry, 11
Cold Harbor, 66
Confederates, 20, 22
Constitution, 7, 8, 86
Copperheads, 46
Corinth, 33
Cross Keys, 38

Davis, Jefferson, 20, 23, 33, 39, 45, 62, 68, 75, 77, 78, 84
Democrats, 15, 17, 72

Douglas, Stephen, 11, 15, 17

Early, General J. A., 70, 71
Emancipation, Proclamation of, 46–8
Ewell, General, 53, 54

Farragut, Admiral, 34, 69
Federals, 20, 23
Fort Donelson, 33
Fort Henry, 33
Fort Monroe, 34–6, 84
Fort No. 10, 33
Fort Republic, 38
Fort Sumter, 20, 21, 81
Fredericksburg, 48, 49
Fremont, 26, 27

Garrison, William Lloyd, 12
Gettysburg, 53–7
Gladstone, W. E., 45
Gordonsville, 40, 41
Grand Gulf, 58, 59
Grant, General Ulysses, 33, 58–61, 63–7, 70, 72, 75, 77, 80, 81, 84
Great Debates, 15, 16
Greeley, Horace, 63

Halleck, General H. W., 33, 40, 42, 49, 60, 70
Harper's Ferry, 12, 23, 31, 42, 44
Hill, General, 53, 54
Hood, General J. B., 68
Hooker, General J., 49, 53, 60

Jackson, General "Stonewall", 38–42, 44, 49, 51
James River, 34, 35, 50
Johnson, President Andrew, 71, 72, 84
Johnston, General Albert Sidney, 31, 33

INDEX

Johnston, General Joseph E., 36, 39, 41, 58, 64, 68, 81–4

Kansas-Nebraska Act, 11, 12, 15
Ku-Klux-Klan, 88

Lincoln, Abraham, youth, 14; inauguration, 18; assassination, 81
Lincoln, Mary, 29, 30
Lee, General Robert E., 23, 39–45, 48, 49, 53, 54, 56, 64–7, 75, 77, 80, 84
Longstreet, General, 41, 53, 54, 60, 62
Louisiana Purchase, 11

Malvern Hill, 40
Manassas, 23, 24, 41
Maryland, 18, 23, 42
Mason, 28
McClellan, General G., 22, 24, 26, 30, 34–40, 42, 44, 45, 72
McDowell, General I., 24, 34, 38
Meade, General G. G., 54, 56, 64
Mechanicsville, 39
Merrimac, the, 35, 36
Missouri Compromise, 11
Mobile, 69, 70
Monitor, the, 35, 36

Nashville, 72

Pemberton, General, 58, 59
Petersburg, 67, 75, 77, 78
Pickett, General G., 54, 56
Pope, General, 33, 40–2
Port Hudson, 59
Potomac, Army of, 24, 31, 34, 64
Presidential Elections, 17, 71

Republicans, 15, 17, 72
Richmond, 23, 34, 38, 39, 40, 48, 53, 66, 75, 78

Rosecrans, General, 59, 60, 64

Scott, Dred, 12
Scott, General Winfield, 23, 24
Secession, 19, 20, 22
Sedgwick, General, 49, 51
Seven Days, battle of, 40
Seven Pines, 39
Seward, W. H., 17, 23, 46, 49, 82
Shenandoah Valley, 38, 70, 72
Sheridan, General P. H., 66, 70, 71, 77, 80
Sherman, General W. T., 33, 58–61, 64, 66, 68, 69, 82–4
Shields, General, 38
Shiloh, 33
Slavery, 8–10, 15, 46–8, 74
Slidell, 28
Spotsylvania, 65
Stanton, E. M., 31, 35, 62, 81
Stephens, Alexander, 75, 76
Stevens, Thaddeus, 18, 46
Stoneman, General, 49
Stowe, Harriet Beecher, 10
Stuart, General J. E. B., 39, 49, 51, 53, 70
Sumner, Charles, 12, 27, 46

Taney, Chief Justice, 12, 19, 84
Territories, the, 3
Thomas, General G. E., 60, 61, 64, 68, 72, 84
Trent, the, 28
Turner's Gap, 42

Vicksburg, 58

West Virginia, 22, 23
White House, 38, 40
Williamsburg, 38
Welles, 35, 59

York River, 34, 36
Yorktown, 36

For Product Safety Concerns and Information please contact our EU
representative GPSR@taylorandfrancis.com
Taylor & Francis Verlag GmbH, Kaufingerstraße 24, 80331 München, Germany

www.ingramcontent.com/pod-product-compliance
Lightning Source LLC
Chambersburg PA
CBHW052131010526
44113CB00034B/1805